WRITE WITHOUT THE FIGHT

MASTER YOUR CREATIVE PROCESS TO WRITE WITH MORE EASE AND SATISFACTION

Other Titles by the Author

Sex, Lies & Creativity, Gender Differences in Creative Thinking (Difference Press, 2014)

Motherhood to Otherhood, Step Up to the New You, Use the Lessons Learned as a Mom to Create a New Life (Running Press, 2008)

RV There Yet? A Cross-Country Cautionary Tale (BookSurge, 2005)

WRITE
WITHOUT
THE FIGHT

*Master Your Creative Process to Write
with More Ease and Satisfaction*

by Julia Roberts, MSc Creativity

*With a Foreword by Joel Madison, Peabody Award winner,
member WGA, SAG, and the Television Academy*

DECODING CREATIVITY

Mightly Little Books is an imprint of Decoding Creativity.com

Decoding Creativity.com is a dba of Julia Roberts LLC, located in North Hills, CA

ISBN/paperback: 979-8-9861423-0-2
ISBN/ebook: 979-8-9861423-1-9
Cover photo: Alashi, I-stock photos,
https://alashinow.wordpress.com
Cover design: Cecily Roberts

DEDICATION

To the Mighty Writers who seek to write their best, but don't need it to be easy. We don't suffer writer's block lying down. We do something about it. (Because we can.)

We are MIGHTY!

I'm so grateful to have your energy in my life!

LIST OF TABLES

TABLE OF CONTENTS

FOREWORD

If you're reading this forward, you're either procrastinating from getting some writing done, you have writers block or maybe like me you are fascinated by the thought that there is a science behind creativity.

Maybe you are like a colleague of mine who says he's never gotten writers block, ever. He told me with great deal of pride. Yet, when pressed, this colleague admitted that the first line of writing is the most difficult for him, sometimes holding him up for days, sometimes for weeks. He didn't want to label it anything. I guess not labeling it writers block was a badge of honor. I didn't have the heart to tell him different, he was already mad at me for the notes I gave him on his script.

Regardless of why you're reading this, congratulations! As soon as you get past this forward you can really dive into this fascinating field of study. And you are about to learn something, about yourself, that will make you a better writer.

So, a little bit about me. I was a professional standup comedian for about 15 years before making a pivot into writing for TV and movies, which I've been doing since 1990. Doing standup was great for a champion procrastinator like myself. Writing for TV, not so much. Suddenly, I had actual deadlines to deal with and people that would be very mad if I did not meet them. No time for any procrastination or writers block except for of course I did wait till the last minute and do all nighters just like in college. For most of my career it wasn't fun. Until I started figuring out that this was my process. The years I could have saved beating myself up if I had known that somehow, I should be involved in the writing process and not try and write like my office mate who could just sit there at the keyboard for twelve hours and finish his task with some time to spare. That was their way. That is what worked for them. Secretly they were beating themselves up as well.

I met Julia several years ago at a writers' conference in Ohio. I was there doing a craft workshop on screenwriting and to a lesser degree comedy screenwriting. It was at one of the lunches that we happened to be sitting at a table together and the subject came up about standup comedy and improv comedy. I was saying that although I had done standup professionally for many years before writing for TV, I was terrible at improv. Without missing a beat Julia said, "that's because one is divergent thinking and the other is convergent thinking." I thought wow, there's an actual scientific reason that I'm bad at it. I found that fascinating.

I do some teaching and workshops on craft and craft is not science, it's nuts, and bolts. It does not take the "instrument", you, into consideration. I started doing a deep dive into what Julia was teaching. I never really thought about that part of it. But like a light bulb it clicked. Of course, you, the individual, needs to be included in the writing process. Sure, you need to know your craft. Without it the structure falls apart and you won't be taken seriously in your field. But what gets you back to the keyboard, to keep moving forward to inspire you or light the creative fire? The answer is you. What Julia teaches goes way beyond craft and focuses on that.

A few years ago, I was teaching a course on sitcom writing at the Columbia College of Chicago. They had a program called semester in Los Angeles. The course guided eager students through writing their first "spec" script and then upon graduation, hopefully helped get them involved in the movie and television industry. I've always been a big proponent of process. Understanding your process is essential to being a better writer. But until I came across creativity as a science all I could really say is that there is a thing called process and good luck finding one that works for you, let's get back to craft.

To my great luck Julia had recently moved to Los Angeles and I was able to get her to give a talk to my class. They were blown away. I know I was. No one had presented creativity in this way before. And it might have been years till they discovered it on their own. It gave them a lot of motivation and really helped them see that they were part of the equation and that they had to be worked on as much as the nuts and bolts of the craft. It gave them the tools to not beat themselves up when they got stuck or struggle as much looking at the blank page. It allowed them room to pause and think about themselves.

Truth be told, I wanted to hear more from Julia and learn some tools to understand why I will do anything in the world rather than put pen to paper. Writing is hard, why would anyone want to do anything this hard? Oh, I still procrastinate but I have a better understanding why.

~ *Joel Madison*

Peabody Award winner; Member WGA, SAG and The Televsion Academy. Story Editor, *Roseanne*, Supervising Producer, *Fresh Prince of Bel-Air*, Co-Exec/Exec Producer, *Malcolm & Eddie* and Consulting Producer, *Crashing*

WELCOME WRITERS!

I'm glad you picked up this book! It means you're my kind of people – weirdos, or, as we're more commonly known, writers. Writers are the best kind of weirdos. We have odd ideas and unique points of view. We see the world differently, which is why we feel compelled to write – something new, surprising, interesting...creative.

I hope *Write Without the Fight* will be a real game-changer for you. It is for the thousands of participants who join me in the Write Without the Fight online course and/or the WWTF Challenge. Just think what you could write if you subtracted your doubt, delay, and resistance. What if you knew exactly what it would take to end your procrastination and get you back to writing, excited and glad to be there?

When you feel better about your writing, you write better.

That's why I'm so excited. Your ideas, commentary, stories, songs, jokes and more are going to flow better, feel better, and *land* better. And I firmly believe your writing will help make the world better, too.

The world needs our voices.

We see things differently. We have opinions and worldviews, that are, well, weird. This is precisely *why* the world needs us. We influence people to see things anew, to solve problems, to empathize with characters and situations. We have stories in our heads that need to be told.

Some of us feel it is somehow modest to question our talent and whether anyone will ever read or care about what we write. But there is an arrogance to that way of thinking.

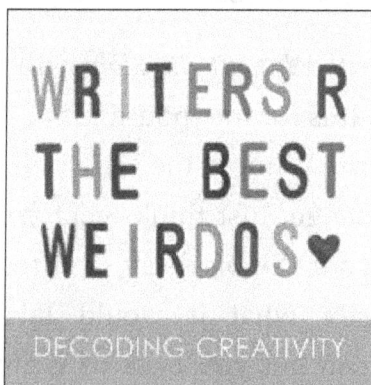

WRITERS R
THE BEST
WEIRDOS♥

DECODING CREATIVITY

Who are you to know what the world will think of your writing? Of your messages and ideas? Is it any less arrogant to be certain no one will care than it is to be certain you're going write a blockbuster hit? You cannot know how your work will be received, and you cannot know who it will connect with and help. To believe otherwise is arrogant. It just is. So, you write, and leave the judgment to the readers. Put a pin in talent. You can't know your level of talent. Write in service of the reader, and your best work will come forth. (That is where modesty belongs. You write to serve.)

This book lays out the best science known to help creators create at their best. For about 70 years, scientists, and creativity practitioners like myself, have been researching, experimenting, and observing creative thought processes, and developing best practices for better creative thinking. And the key learning is that we each have different creative thinking strengths – and we each struggle in different phases of the thinking process! This explains why…

"Writer's block" is different for each of us.

Some people insist writer's block is a myth. (Bully for them.) But writer's block-deniers don't realize that it's real and painful for many of us, even if they seem to be blessedly asymptomatic. Using science, we can diagnose the cause and timing of your own type of writer's block, and essentially vaccinate you against it. You can become adept at using the tools that help you find your clarity, ideas, structure and finish your creative projects.

Write Without the Fight FB Group

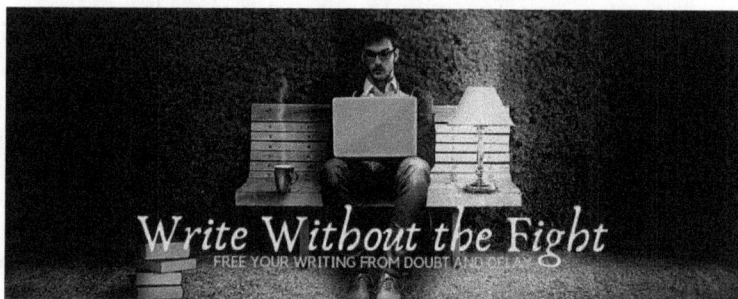

You don't have to do it alone.

You can do it with us. We weirdos need each other. But where do weirdos gather to feel safe in their weirdness? The *Write Without the Fight* private, free FB Group, (https://www.facebook.com/groups/wwtfgroup) of course. There, you are in exactly the right place to find a supportive community of absolutely incredible writers who *get it*, and who are striving to get the fight out of their writing process.

Write Without the Fight is a free, active, private FB group where writers of all kinds gather and discuss concepts about creativity, writing, our process and more. Come join, ask a question, tell us what trips you up. This is where stuck writers go to get unstuck. (I've got a hack for that!)

Mighty Writers

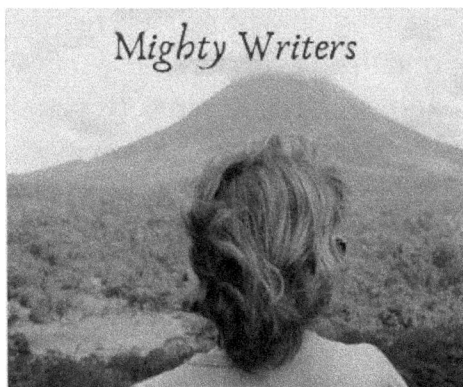

In the group, I feature blogs (yours and mine), discuss issues we face as writers, and have some writerly fun.

We periodically take up the Write Without the Fight Challenge. In 2020, we had several mini-writing retreats, a dream interpretation session, and our first office party on Zoom, which included hand dancing, door prizes, and a Dickensian drinking game. To sign up for the next challenge, go to: https://go.decodingcreativity.com/5-day

Write Without the Fight is where you go to begin your journey to write with more ease and satisfaction.

The Mighty Writers Club

In addition, there's the Mighty Writers Club, which is a coaching and writing club. We write together almost daily and meet regularly for group coaching. Here's where you can get feedback, reframe an issue, get new ideas and training on writing and creativity topics like how to plan, or organize your writing. And we work on building your audience as you write. (If you'd like to learn more, go here: https://go.decodingcreativity.com/mighty.)

As I mentioned, we write as a group almost daily! This gets you "back in the game," as one of my clients said the other day.

The Mighty Writers Club has its own virtual "clubhouse" where you'll find an abundance of creativity DIY programs, recorded sessions, interviews with authors, agents, industry experts etc., so you can find the help you need when you need it on topics like:

- How to find an agent

- The creative thinking process

- How much you might earn for your book

- How to self-publish

- The four-act story structure

- How to publish traditionally

You feel connected, accountable ... and you're writing.

The Mighty Writers Club is designed to be affordable, so you can achieve what you need, writing-wise, even if it takes a year or more. Some of my writers are entering their third year with me and are in the publishing phase. We'd love to welcome you into the club.

You can also ask for help with a problem and get it, right then and there. You have your own exclusive FB group for paid club members, where you know the people, and you belong. You can ask for help, celebrate, vent, or brag. If you're ready, you can join us and get writing, build your audience, and learn more about how you create and write (and why you sometimes don't).

I hope you enjoy the book, and I hope it helps get you writing again, with less fear and resistance and more ease and satisfaction.

~ Julia Roberts, MSc

DECODING CREATIVITY

P.S. I share a model of creative thinking called Deliberate Creativity, based on earlier scientific models of creative thinking, especially the Foursight Model of Creative Thinking.[i] I've tweaked my model to be more writer/creator-friendly. I've also curated and adjusted proven creativity tools to better help writers. The science is credited, open-source and cited research in the scientific peer-reviewed literature under the names Creative Problem Solving, and CPS. I cite tools' origins in the Endnotes, based on Creative Education Foundation language.

I share this to ground your understanding of these tools and theories in the deep wealth of research, experimentation, and observation they come from, and to give credit and show respect for my community of creativity practitioners.

WHEN YOU MAKE MUSIC OR WRITE OR CREATE, IT'S REALLY YOUR JOB TO HAVE MIND-BLOWING, IRRESPONSIBLE, CONDOMLESS SEX WITH WHATEVER IDEA IT IS YOU'RE WRITING ABOUT AT THE TIME.

~LADY GAGA

1ˢᵀ STEP – SEE THE PROBLEM

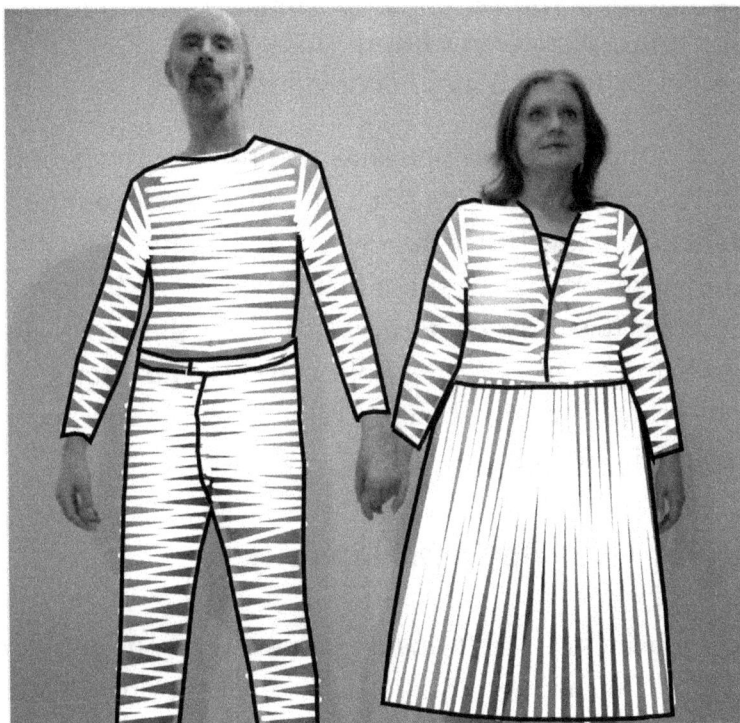

1 "What you see you think" by Trevor Butcher - Artist_ CC BY 2.0

SEE THE PROBLEM: WHY NO ONE CARES ABOUT YOUR WRITER'S BLOCK

- *It's Not their Business, Literally*
- *Whose Business is It?*
- *If They Talked About It, They'd Have to Fix It (And They Don't Know How)*
- *A Different Way of Looking at It*

Writer's block is personal, painful, your own kind of hell. To everyone else, it's just a nuisance. Even your family thinks they know better than you why you're not writing – and their theories are just not helpful. Why don't the many industries that rely on writers to create the news copy, advertising, books, scripts, jokes, songs and more –care about your writer's block? Why aren't more people investing in a cure?

It's Not Their Business, Literally

Businesses can't make money on you until you produce finished writing. That's their business. Many talented writers cannot finish a book because of writer's block or other resistance to their writing or creative process. Since this problem is widespread, the industry can only afford to engage in people who write, finish, and present their work for publication or production.

This is true of publishers, producers, agents, and academic programs like journalism and MFAs – they are all "hands off" on writer's block. That's your issue and your responsibility, which implies...it's your fault. And writers feel powerless over writer's block, so, yes, they also feel shame. In order to combat these feelings, they might overeat, overthink or overdrink. More shame and self-blame.

Some people believe that writer's block is laziness. They buy in to publishers' assessment "they don't have what it takes."

Writers block and procrastination are not character flaws.
They're 100% fixable with the right tools at the right time.

But...you might need some help getting unstuck and getting your writing flowing again.

So many writers, so little time. There are plenty of writers to choose from in a pile of finished manuscripts. But are those always the best ideas and stories? If many writers can't write, we'll never know.

If MFA programs and publishers took responsibility for helping writers get over writer's block, what got written and published would indeed shift dramatically.

Whose Business Is It?

Why are there so many books in the world? Because writing is a calling. And writers have a pressing story to tell, or character to try out, a world to build, or expertise to share.

People have a leftover belief from the days of vanity presses. They think "if you have to pay, it's not 'real.'" And writing is "free," and if you're any good, you "should be able to do it with just pen and paper."

But if that were the case, why are there myriad MFAs, conferences, retreats and writing programs? Why has self-publishing created an explosion of writers investing in themselves and their writing?

Not investing in your inner writer is to deny your creativity, your calling, your self-exploration, your potential for growth. Because creating IS growth. And like any kind of growth, you invest time (and money) in pursuing it or avoiding it.

Avoiding it is often more costly.

People feel permission to spend on conferences and MFAs because they are improving their craft. But they don't feel it is "right" to spend on improving their instrument – themselves, their ideas, or their creative thinking process.

In fact, they hope if they invest in craft, there will be some nugget of information that will relieve them of their problems when writing – something will lock into place si they can just write, without the fight and resistance they have always come up against.

You can ask your friends and teachers for advice, and even well-intentioned people give bad advice, or advice that works for them, but not necessarily for you.

You end up feeling even worse – like it must really be your fault. And there must really be no cure for this. If you were any good, you'd just…

- Have a clear vision of your book from start to finish

- Have great, exciting, motivating, original ideas

- Be able to stick it out through the murky middle and perfect your work

- Have finishing energy, and be eager to bring it to market

If They Talked About It, They'd Have to Fix It (And They Don't Know How)

Agents, editors, producers, publishers, and writing programs have a profit motive for maintaining the status quo. As we've said, there is no good business rationale to swim in the deep end and help writers who are drowning in doubt and delay. Why bother, when finished – even if imperfect – books and scripts are washing up on shore every day, and all they have to do is pick one up, have a beach read, and run their profitable businesses?

And what if, one day, there were no good books to scavenge among the finished material? They still wouldn't know how to help the writers in the deep end. As a business matter, it is better not to address them, because then they might have to fix it and they don't know how.

A Different Way of Looking at It

The industry is all about how to write better. And we all HOPE that is what is wrong with us – we're just not good enough – because that we might be able to fix. We hope – and believe, and spend money on the chance that – if we're *earnest,* we'll complete something. We can learn, try, do and fix ourselves.

I don't teach craft. The entire industry is aimed at improving the craft of writing, because it is the only thing 99% of teachers know how to tackle. My business, Decoding Creativity, switches the focus.

I focus on the instrument – you.

- How you think, how you create, and what gets in your way

- What conditions you need to succeed and create at your best

- Where your creativity will be valued, and where you'll value creating and sharing your work

For me and my clients, it is finally obvious. The craft is important, but the instrument is paramount. Without a working "instrument," no amount of sheet music will help you create. You are the instrument. Sometimes you work, and sometimes you're flat or sharp, or just not working.

But if you – the instrument – need help, craft lessons will not suffice. There is absolutely nothing wrong with you. You might need a good tuning, or different atmospheric conditions, but you are the writer - the instrument.

It is you who makes the noise, has the ideas, writes the work. It is you, yourself, who deserves caring and maintenance.

What you need is to shift your focus from craft to instrument. Who are you creatively? How do you think? What and when are you blocked? Why?

We need your voice and contribution to get out of your head and onto paper. Share your insights and save the world. One book, one essay, song, poem, headline, script, story, or joke at a time.

When it comes to getting advice from other writers, people share what works for them. They say:

- Set a schedule and write every day

- Brainstorm new ideas

- Just get over it – it's all in your head

- Smile, buddy, you'll get there

- Write anything. Just write.

- Shake it off

- Relax

- Drink

When these pearls of wisdom don't work for you, you feel doubly shamed.

Decoding Creativity relies on scientifically sound assessments to draw a clear image of how you think. We name your creative thinking strengths and help you face your creative thinking struggles. We prescribe the appropriate tools and methods for you to address your block. This book gives you a simple approach to understanding who you are creatively. It is best to seek professional assessment – but if you choose not to, we're going to get you a strong start.

You are a certain kind of blocked, and once we know what kind, we have the right Rx.

Maria Archer, painter, cartoonist...

creates her art for family and. For her, painting and writing have their own rewards.

As Maria shared, "I was holding myself back. I've always had the sense I was holding myself back. And it was frustrating. Years and years of therapy gave me less insight into how I create than working with Julia."

WRITING IS SOLITARY. IS HELP HELPFUL?

- *Is it Possible to Help Someone Else Write Better?*
- *Unblock Your Block - But How?*
- *Will This Work For You?*

Is It Possible to Help Someone Else Write Better?

Is writing a talent? An inborn gift that no one can take away from you?

There's a lot of debate about whether writing is a skill or a talent. And for me, it is both. Everyone writes, and everyone learns the skill in school. You can hardly keep a job without at least occasionally writing... at least an invoice.

But some of us *love* writing. And as a result, we improve our skills and hope that our brains, ideas, and turns-of-phrase might just be different enough to get us recognized as a talent.

If you are simply skilled, you can serve a great many people with your writing. If you're talented, your writing might move and/or entertain millions of people.

Q: What is a talent?

A: Something that separates you from other skilled practitioners – athletic, creative, or entrepreneurial, for example, whether it is by way of style, ability, skill, or passion.

For me, and for the writers I work with, writing is a calling. Whether their writing remains a hobby, is shared with a small audience, is published or produced, or becomes a bestselling book or blockbuster hit, they will write.

And, when they're not writing, they have the recurring thought: *I should write…*

Martha Beck, NYT bestseller and Oprah Book Club author, and Oprah Magazine Columnist

trained me as a life coach in 2008. As my training ended, Martha offered this gem: "Julia wields great insight and talent. Because of her humor, fresh point of view, and intelligence she will provide great service to the lucky people who seek her out."

Would you continue to write, even if you knew you'd never get published?

View Insights   455 Post Reach >

I recently asked this question in the Write Without the Fight FB group. There was not a "no" among the responses. Two comments said they need to *believe* publishing was an option, or they'd stop. But otherwise, it was a universal, "YES."

So, there is skill, there is calling, and if you're lucky, there is talent.

Absent a brain injury, everyone's writing can improve over time through experience, life and various activities, including:

- Reading

- Writing and writing classes

- Critique

- Practice

- And… growing self-awareness

This book, my work, and the discussions in the Write Without the Fight FB Group are all geared toward the last point – self-knowledge and gaining access to your best writing. (Join @https://fb.com/groups/WWTFgroup).

Craft vs. Instrument

As we've discussed, most writers spend time and money on craft – writing retreats, classes, conferences – and well they should, since there is a lot to learn and hone. But they spend very little time on themselves as writers.

If playing the instrument is the territory of "craft," then you are the instrument.

Practicing scales and learning fancy finger work – craft – is not sufficient. You need to know the ins and outs of the instrument. You need the finest instrument, and to know how to get the finest music from the one you have.

> *You can write your best when you know what kind of instrument you are as a writer.*

- Who are you as a writer, as a creator?

- Where do you get hamstrung?

- When does the work come easily to you? Give you bursts of energy?

- Where/when does it feel like a slog? Like you'll never be able to do it?

These are, to extend the instrument metaphor, your high notes and low notes. Your range, if you will.

TRY IT

Stop reading and close your eyes (once you finish this paragraph, of course). Think about a couple of projects for which you had great enthusiasm but never finished.

Think... Remember the projects...Write them down.

1.
2.
3.
4.
5.

Now, visit each project in your memory (again, closing your eyes) and relive what felt vital and exciting, and where and when the project lost steam.

Try not to let the crutch of "I didn't have time" define why you walked away from them. At the very least, you didn't think it was "worth the time," but we all have time to do things that are exciting, challenging, and compelling. What/when was it you lost the sense that this work was worth it? When did you lose faith in it? When did you stop believing that it was going to be great? That it was fun and interesting?

Write down what part of the process bogged you down and made you drift or walk away from the project.

Did you...

1. LOSE THE VISION?

2. RUN OUT OF IDEAS?

3. GET OVERWHELMED BY ITS COMPLEXITY?

4. COULDN'T FINISH; DIDN'T SEE THE PATH TO PUBLICATION/PRODUCTION

Those all feel like "your fault" right? Like you're the only person in the world who could have fixed what you were writing if only you'd had: 1) A clear vision, 2) a brilliant idea, 3) weren't so lazy, or were just plain good enough or 4) were rescued by an agent, publisher, or producer.

In the next chapter, we're going to learn more about Deliberate Creativity and how you can understand what parts of the creative thinking process give you energy and which parts bog you down.

Gaining this knowledge of the process, and your relationship to it, will give you significant insight into what it will take for you – the instrument – to create what you envision. From idea to draft to a finished manuscript to published or produced, you are the common thread. You are the creative constant, so it is all about how you fit or fight the universal creative process.

These insights into your instrument - how you write and when you quit - can be used deliberately to drive your work forward! Exciting?

So, we repeat the question...*Can someone else help you write at your best?* Yes. As many geniuses as there are, published and produced, there are likely an equal number who are stymied and frustrated.

Even geniuses need creative confidence – and not just once, but over and over again. And how could self-awareness, self-acceptance, and validation make such a difference? We're going to look at that phenomenon.

What might inspire creative confidence in you?

Inspiration is... feeling primed to get back to it! Excited to create. That is the domain of mindset. And it contributes not just to when or if you write, but if you're able to write your best work. *Write Without the Fight* is designed to be that muse to your writing. It's a way to hold you up, against all odds, when you sag.

Write Without the Fight is a guide, hack, pal, ear, mirror, and armchair expert when you need one.

Unblock Your Block - But How?

There is one kind of self-knowledge that is usually not available to writers. We may come to understand all sorts of things about ourselves and how to write with the weird mix of optimism/ambivalence, vision/detail, perspective/empathy, and introvert/extrovert that jumble inside us, hoping to form sentences, create characters, build worlds, and capture audiences. But very few of us are offered precise insight into what goes on in our brains.

We need to know…

- Why do we resist? What can help alleviate that resistance?

- How does creative thinking operate?

- How can we master it?

When it's all humming along, we think we're brilliant. When it comes to a halt, we blame ourselves.

Our inner voices yell at us:

"Lazy. Stupid. Arrogant."

"Who do you think you are?"

"Quit procrastinating and get it done!"

Sometimes we see it and call it what it is: BLOCKED. Often, we think it is a character flaw, unfixable. This self-judgment and self-blame can deepen the block.

Is there a simple trick that can unblock the block?

Creative studies, a branch of psychology, has a full body of scientific literature dedicated to how humans create. Within that body of research, observation, and

experimentation, lies the secret you need to unblock your own block.

The reason this vital information hasn't found its way into mainstream understanding is good news and bad.

The bad news is, it's complicated and personal. *(What about writing isn't?)* It takes some assessment – whether self-assessment or professional – to know what fix will work for you. And there are *many* fixes. It takes time and practice to find your fixes and learn to use them effectively.

The good news is – it is known and knowable. We know how to predict your block, prevent it, and pull you forward when you hit the wall. Block doesn't have to be as mysterious or painful as it is reputed to be.

Mary Stiers Miller, singer/songwriter and comedian...

is enthusiastic, energetic and contagiously happy.

But not always... One day she told us she was frozen in her tracks. She has fairly constant writing deadlines, and no matter how she feels when she's writing, it's gotta be fun and funny when she delivers it.

"Julia totally broke through a serious block I created around my writing, that had me frozen in my tracks. After talking with her, my writing flowed again."

You know not just that you're brilliant but HOW you're brilliant.

Let me share an idea with you that instantly deflates resistance and overwhelm. It is so simple that it's deceptive. Try it tomorrow when you're looking at your to-do list.

TRY IT

Write out your to-do list – in its fullest iteration. Get all your thoughts and expectations on to that list.

- Look at that list… How does it make you feel? Where do you feel the resistance?

- Now, take the list, and scratch out "To-Do" and write in "Might-Do" instead.

- It becomes your Might-Do list.

Doesn't that feel better already? You *might* do these things. You might do them all. You might not. It all feels like a choice. It all feels more possible.

You'll see more about the word "might" in the Clarity tools in the Don't-Get-Stopped-in-Your-Tracks Hacks section. "Might" has been shown to reduce resistance in our brains. It's simple, effective, and grounded in research, experiments, and observations of hundreds of practitioners and thousands of creative subjects. And wouldn't you like better ideas?

"CREATIVITY REQUIRES THE COURAGE TO LET GO OF CERTAINTIES."

~ ERICH FROMM

Will It Work for You?

Learning the basics of the creative thinking process is proven to enhance idea sessions – in both quality and quantity of ideas.[ii]

Understanding how you think is powerful help. It's like knowing the combination to your locker in high school. If you didn't know the code, how long might you spin the dial and try to open that lock? Is that opening the lock? Or is it just trying?

Do you want to write or just *try to write*?

It is simple to learn your creative thinking profile. Once you know, you begin to find the right hacks and tools for you. You build the habit of recognizing when you need help, and what help to seek. You begin, with support, to *learn your locker combination.*

Join the FREE Write Without the Fight FB group and participate. We discuss a creativity concept each week and work to remove resistance to your writing goals.

How to Tell if You're Blocked, Lazy or Just Scared

- *What is Blocked?*
- *What is Lazy?*
- *Is Scared Sacred?*

What is Blocked?

Why, again, aren't you writing? Sometimes, it's quite specific... like: *I'm taking a break before I start the rewrite.* More often, it is drifting... like: *I'm going to get back to that,* or, *As soon as ....* *I'm definitely going to...* and after a while, it's *I'm too busy to write.*

Sometimes you have a whole night to yourself, and you say you're going to write, but instead you binge watch a season of *The Bachelor.* Is it safe to call that "lazy?" Maybe. Maybe not. Is that scared? Only you can know, and even then, only if you really get in touch with what is making you stop or stall. It is hard to make sense of why you're not writing – even though you want to. It can be painful, right?

> ### _Laurie Stephans, award-winning comedy writer..._
>
> "_Write Without the Fight_ helped me understand the creative thinking process and showed me what I thought was procrastination was just me being stuck in the part of the process that came most naturally to me. This realization, along with Julia's clear process for working with both strengths and struggles, provided both insight and inspiration to me as a writer."

Simply put, writer's block is the inability to write – start, continue, finish – even though you want to. You feel unable to write with satisfaction, sometimes even if you sit down at your desk day after day.

Writer's block is all in your head. I'm not suggesting it's not real, I just mean the problem is literally located in your head. When you feel bad – because of your fears, judgments, worries, doubts, and expectations – you begin to shame yourself. Emotion downshifts your thinking locus from the neo-cortex to the limbic (or emotional) area, also called the "dog brain." If you're downright scared, it shifts all the way down to the reptilian brain, a.k.a. the "lizard brain" or "gator brain." (See _The Triune Brain,_ below.)

Operating from this emotional thinking center can literally shut down your ability to write. The complexity of the world you are trying to create can overwhelm you. The ideas you come up with can seem lame and disappointing. You're stuck, hopeless, and worthless – among other emotional responses this condition might evoke for you. It can last minutes, days, even years. The longer it lasts the more fear you might experience as you try to break the block and write again.

White-knuckling your way through "block" won't usually fix it. You need to upshift the center of your thinking by deliberately changing your energy and mood. Upshifting is consciously lifting the nexus of your thinking from the lizard or dog brain to the story brain. We'll discuss many hacks for upshifting[iii]/downshifting and mastering your creative process in the pages ahead.

Table 1: *The Triune Brain – Our Brains Evolved in Three Layers.*[iv]

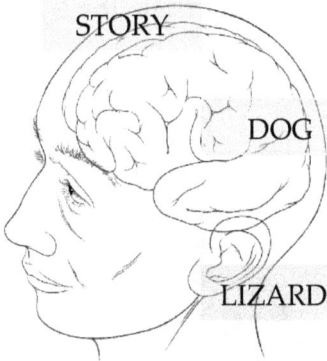

STORY BRAIN is ego, complex thinking, where stories are generated – to explain the world, our feelings, and to tell a story. (a.k.a. the neo-cortex)

DOG BRAIN is pure feeling. Like a dog, it is happy, sad, mad, or afraid without apology or explanation. (a.k.a. the limbic system)

LIZARD BRAIN - Our first and most rudimentary brain. Survival-mode (a.k.a. the reptilian brain)

You're in very good company.

Writer's block is well-documented psychological condition, publicly claimed and shared by writers like: Elizabeth Gilbert, F. Scott Fitzgerald, Charles M. Schulz, Rachmaninoff, and Adele. Herman Melville never wrote again after *Moby-Dick,* but not for lack of trying. *To Kill a Mockingbird,* masterpiece that it is, was Harper Lee's only published work for 55 years. (*Go Set a Watchman, 2015*)

One of the earliest complainers of "block" was Russian Impressionist painter, Leonid Pasternak 1862-1945 father to Boris Pasternak, Nobel prize winner and author of *Doctor Zhivago.*

2 Figure: public domain, cc license

How to Stop Procrastinating

All my clients complain of procrastinating. That's what they want help with, more than any other obstacle. Procrastinating stands between them and glory.

They see it as a character flaw. A bad habit that I might beat out of them. They hear their mothers', teachers', and boss's voices scolding them for procrastinating.

From where I sit, procrastination is fixable with the right tool at the right time. And it is definitely not mere laziness. It is often painful; you feel powerless to fix it. Procrastination is an utter loss of energy – often just as you're required to face your most challenging creative thinking phase. No wonder you feel overwhelmed and barely have the energy to eat a cookie, watch TV, or play a video game. Which feels better in the short term, a cookie and some entertainment? Or an unrelenting thinking challenge that drains you of energy?

"YOU ARE BETTER THAN YOU THINK YOU ARE."

~ ERMA BOMBECK

What is Lazy?

By definition, lazy means unwilling to work or expend energy. Relaxing could be seen as lazy behavior. But "lazy" can also be a calculation of what's "worth" doing.

The implication of lazy – and all the emotional crap that word heaps onto your soul – is that you're unwilling to work for *specious reasons*. Lazy is 100% judgeable. So, when you're berating yourself as "lazy," it is not likely that you think there's a perfectly good reason you're not willing to do the work.

Judgment makes it emotional, which downshifts your thinking to the dog or lizard brain and makes the complexity of what you're trying to write suddenly overwhelming. If you can, upshift. Do what it takes to feel good again, and then get back to it.

You can't progress – or upshift – until you stop judging yourself. Maybe, banish the word "lazy" from your vocabulary. There are times when you're just tired. Sometimes you need a break. Many of us permit rest and relaxation for others, but not for ourselves. If you have a hard time justifying recreation or just lolling around, take a minute and ask yourself, are you lazy? Are the expectations in play reasonable? Realistic?

There's an Expectation, Lurking

Much of the time, our moods are regulated by our expectations. The general wisdom is...

"SHOOT FOR THE MOON. EVEN IF YOU MISS IT YOU WILL LAND AMONG THE STARS."

~LES BROWN

Expectations can be tricky. When I grew up, that motto was emblazoned on posters in every guidance counselor's office. And we all wanted to *shoot for the moon*. Otherwise, what were you? A loser? Lazy? Well, as I said, expectations lurk behind most of our feelings. And they can be too high or too low. And other people's expectations of you can shape who you become. (See Table 2: *How Expectations Shape Our Moods and Reactions)*

Malcolm Gladwell, author of five *New York Times* bestsellers, speaker and podcaster, says of writer's block and expectations:

Expectations are just thoughts. If you're suffering from high – or low – expectations, look at the havoc that mere thought can have on your approach to work.

Expectations can really hold you hostage. Let them go. Let yourself tackle the desired project, in teeny tiny baby steps… or maybe slow and steady turtle steps. Make your expectations so easy that your body relaxes, and you think, "It's so easy even I can do it."

"I DEAL WITH WRITER'S BLOCK BY LOWERING MY EXPECTATIONS. I THINK THE TROUBLE STARTS WHEN YOU SIT DOWN TO WRITE AND IMAGINE THAT

YOU WILL ACHIEVE SOMETHING
MAGICAL AND MAGNIFICENT — AND
WHEN YOU DON'T, PANIC SETS IN.

NEVER TRY TO BE THE HARE. ALL HAIL
THE TORTOISE."

~ MALCOLM GLADWELL

Table 2: *How Expectations Shape Our Moods and Reactions*

If expectations	Are Too High	Are Too Low
For yourself	You can shut down, resist, try and fail; avoid goal setting because of the pain it induces	You can under-perform and/or suffer low self-esteem
For others	They can abdicate responsibility/agency; feel ill-equipped to take on challenges successfully	They can under-perform, or seek another mentor who expects better of them
Others' of you	You feel stressed, resentful, feel like a fraud	You feel hurt, withdrawn, undervalued

But What If, YES, You're Just Being Lazy?

Sometimes you just don't wanna. (*Whine.*) And "don't wanna" is when you're most likely to scold yourself for laziness. Is "don't wanna" a specious reason to be unwilling to work? Maybe. You've got to dig in a little, and ask yourself:

Why don't you want to do it?

Is it something you must do?

Is there a way to make it easier, more palatable?

Is bullying yourself really going to work?

"Don't wanna" can also be a red flag that tells you what you're working on is not really deserving of your talent and voice. It is your integrity *resisting*. This is your laziness *working very hard* to get you to walk away from the project and pick up something that is more urgent for you – closer to your core values, worth your time, energy, and effort.

How to Stop Procrastinating

So, what have we learned about procrastinating? It is often hiding your ego from painful thoughts like

-   "I'm not sure how to proceed"

- "I'm afraid I'm just no good"

- "I don't like what I've written"

The worst thing you can do is to judge the "procrastinating." Let it be. Let it help you forward. Let it become "procrastubation," i.e. a combination of incubation and procrastination. And by all means, examine and lower your expectations.

Is Scared Sacred?

Without realizing it, you may feel scared to write. Writing – taking a stand – claiming the authority of an author, is emotionally risky. Your ego may be serving up a very reasonable rationale for not trying to write – not risking it. You might feel very "grown-up" when you "accept" that you're never going to be an Austen or a Hemingway. This fear can begin to feel not like fear at all, but "reality." It takes on a sacred, inviolable status. Your ego works hard to keep you from peeking behind the curtain to see that the reality you've created is just fear.

Your ego is not unlike that little man from Kansas who was afraid people would find out he was a fraud, so he created the Wizard of Oz, an illusion that fooled others and that he, too, began to believe. By frantically working the levers, creating puffs of smoke and a scary image, he intimidated people into inaction. Scared can begin to feel sacred.

Powerful, fearful thoughts, propped up with snide and belittling comments (like "who do you think you are?" or "yeah, right!") are like the comments of any powerful monarch, clergyman, boss or ex-spouse who uses fear to control you. That power is not sacred.

Your ego seeks to maintain its status and power. It is up to you to topple it and overcome the fears it perpetuates. Like any powerful entity, the ego, if not questioned, can abuse its power. It works to keep you safe, keep you small, and protect the *status quo*. In the mindset of ego, change/risk is never worthwhile, and fear is a strong demotivator.

So, Which are You? Blocked? Scared? or Lazy?

TRY IT

What are you experiencing? What did you feel last time you were stuck, blocked or not writing?

- Are you blocked? In need of rest, rejuvenation, and emotional shift?

- Is your block painful? Are you in fear that it will never end? Do you contribute emotional fuel to the fear and, therefore, the block?

- Are you lazy? A shiftless, no-good, don't-wanna baby who should-be-writing, EVEN if that tripe you're turning out isn't worth the effort?

- Does your fear exert power over you – hoping to reinforce *status quo*?

- Is laziness your pal – your "get out of jail free" card – your way to not notice that what you're working on isn't exactly your calling?

- In fact, lazy and blocked are both judgy, icky states we enter when we are not performing up to expectations. The answer seems not necessarily to perform better, but expect better, with more compassion and curiosity.

  - *Fear is a bully we obey at our own peril.*

Catherine Roberts, founder QOVF.org...

founded Quilts of Valor which has delivered over 300,000 handmade quilts to wounded American warriors.

And she was burnt-out.

"I felt overwhelmed, on the verge of giving up! But Julia has the uncanny ability to home in on 'what ails you' with laser precision. And she does it with humor which had me laughing through those dark valleys of self-doubt and the poor-me's."

SEE THE PROBLEM - RECAP

- No one cares about your writer's block – but that doesn't mean you shouldn't treat your "condition" with some care and attention.

- Just because no one in the industry talks about it, doesn't mean

    o it's not real

    o it's your fault or

    o there's no help or cure out there

- You have to see your craft – writing – and your instrument – you, the writer – separately, and invest in them both.

Creating is growth. Creativity is decodable. (i.e., there's a combination for that lock.) Quit "trying" to write, and just write.

Can you tell if you're block, lazy or scared? Do you have to be able to tell? Quit judging yourself for the struggles in your creative process and get help. You deserve help.

2ND STEP – NAME IT

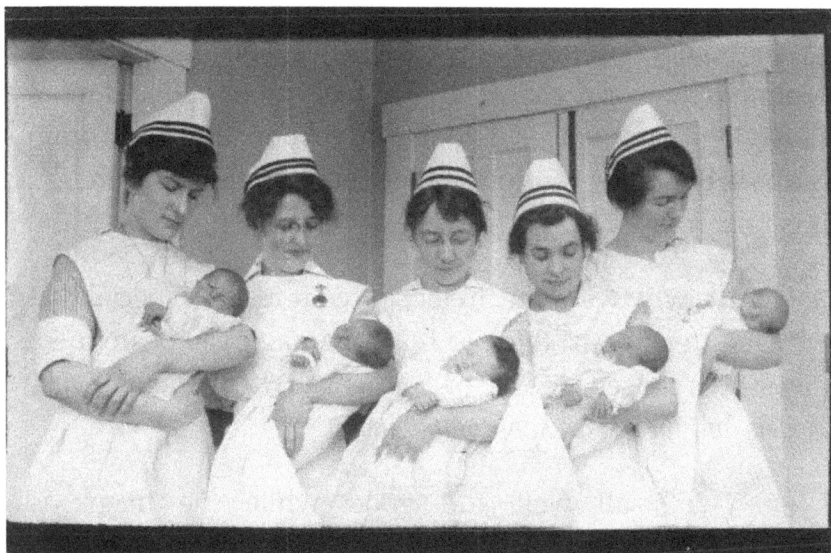

Name the Problem with No Name

- *The Magic and Science of Creativity*
- *Big Magic, "Flow," and the Zone*
- *Science of Creativity*
- *Deliberate Creativity*

The Magic and Science of Creativity

Sometimes when you're writing, you can lose track of time. The world you're writing feels more real and more satisfying than the world you're in, corporeally. Your brain is doing the living for your whole self. It can feel like magic. It is pure joy.

It's why we write. In fact, often it feels so special that we can utterly resist the idea that this magic can be defined, measured, caused, goosed or … scienced. *Keep your formulas, models and theories away from my magic.*

That's all well and good while the magic is happening.

Science is there for when things stall. Or go wrong. Science can bring you back to the magic when it all starts to feel illusory.

Sex is magic and wonderful. And usually, we don't want a doctor in the bedroom. But when things go wrong, or we need diagnostic help, who isn't glad, relieved even, to let science in? We want to fix it and find that magic again. Sometimes, we just need the help of a scientific practitioner to put the magic back in our lives.

Big Magic, Flow, and the Zone

Magic

Elizabeth Gilbert[v] calls it "Big Magic" and when she refers to magic, she means it literally, "like, in the Hogwarts sense...the supernatural." She believes the planet is inhabited by ideas that visit us. When you say "yes," that idea picks you and wants to be made by you. Then, she says, you feel an immediate urgency to make or write or do that thing.

Flow

The late (and great) psychologist Mihalyi Csikszentmihalyi [vi] (pronounced *mi-HI chitz-en-mi HI*) scientifically observed hundreds of creators who described a state of ecstasy when creating that he called "flow." Flow is a state of being in which the work you are doing is so intense and immersive, you can forget that you have bodily needs. You might lose track of time, forget to eat, and write away, in ecstasy. It can feel like magic.

The Zone

Some writers do whatever they can to get in the zone. It's about environment, primarily. Some light a candle, play a certain song or game. Many shut out all distractions, whereas others seek the bustle of a coffee shop or the corner booth at their favorite luncheonette.

When it's not an exterior need, it can be a different kind of need. Some feel the need to eat sweets or salty snacks to juice the muse. Throughout history, writers have been drinkers or drug users. Anything to tame the inner critic and relieve the pressure to write.

There are other methods of getting in the zone, including walking, showering, driving, and shopping. While no one can write *while* doing those things, they are often considered – by writers – essential to getting into the all-mighty zone.

TRY IT

Whether this state-of-being is brought on by magic, mental immersion, or ice cream, it is fleeting and special, and we all want more of it.

- Do you have a superstitious belief about how to find or choose your ideas?

- Do you have lucky underwear?

- Is there a routine that summons your muse?

- Do you believe creative immersion is achieved by magic, you are chosen by an idea?

- Or do you have other superstitions about how you create and how you get into writing?

Most of us do have rituals and beliefs around our creativity, and that is 100% okay. The feeling is intense and personal, so of course we work to protect what we think brings it on.

We don't want to jinx it.

Even if you believe leprechauns brought you your bestselling plot, it needn't detract from the understanding that your mental state can be observed or understood by scientists. (And by *you*.)

And if there's a hack to enter that state of ecstasy, how does that make you feel?

Call it Magic or Flow, either way we say, more please.

John Onorato, writer...

knew about the creative process, "but I didn't know specifically about MY creativity. When I signed up with Julia, I hoped to gain some deeper insights into my own process — and I'm happy to say that it worked.

These new insights and understandings about my own creative process have enabled me to grow and expand as a writer.

It has been a joy establishing a daily writing practice with other people, and I look forward to continuing it in the future. The course has also enabled me to reattach to some works I have in-progress."

The Science of Creativity

Believe it or not, we have the CIA to thank for our deeper understanding of creative thinking. Back in the early 1950's, they understood that creativity helped make a good spy. They could test for strength and agility. They had the new IQ tests to test for intelligence. They wanted a CQ – a creativity quotient. Typical of a government agency, they wanted to be able to give our creativity a number and rank us according to our CQ. They pumped a lot of money into research, and a new branch of psychology was born. Eventually, the quest for the CQ ended, but the research into creative thinking continued to thrive.

We've been developing research, experiments, and theories about creativity for about 70 years. And in that time, we have come to understand a lot about how to enhance, nurture, support, and cause creativity.

We understand how the brain works when it's creating – what the process is, how the thoughts cycle.

We have best practices that can guide you back, reliably, and deliberately, when your magic isn't showing up.

Study after study shows, when Deliberate Creativity and its tools are used, the "magic" also happens. Your best ideas show up in your work in quantity and quality.

A Bit More About Me

As you may know, I have my Masters in the Science of creativity. Yep, I'm that nerd. I needed to understand this creative force in my life that was at once satisfying, self-defining, and at the same time, unbelievably frustrating and hurtful. I wanted to, if not

control, at least steer this energy to create the things I wanted to create. I am grateful there is a science of creativity. It has opened me up to writing the books that are truly mine to write. I can see my particular strengths and what they are best suited to explore and create. And I can see where I struggle, so I can get help instead of feeling helpless and hopeless. Most importantly, I can finish what I start.

Divergent and Convergent Thinking

One of the most fundamental best practices to optimize your creativity is to separate divergent and convergent thinking sessions. (*Huh?* and *What?* I know, *science*.)

Divergent thinking is when you are generating – ideas, content, concepts. It is basically when you're plotting or writing. You are generating something new.

Convergent thinking is selecting and perfecting. It is clarifying, editing or rewriting.

And the basic idea is this: DON'T EDIT AS YOU WRITE. If you do, you're judging as you go, and you'll never reach your best writing or bring forth your best ideas.

Diverging and converging use two different parts of the brain, and if you're constantly shifting from one locus to the other, you never get either "machine" warmed up and working at its best. Diverge first and fully. Then converge. You can interpret this to mean, write a full first draft before you make any changes to your manuscript, or (at the very least) to write/diverge in one session, and then edit/converge in a different session. Don't toggle between the two.

Bill Kenower, author of *Fearless Writing*[vii], says the worst thing that can happen to a writer is the insipid thought:

"Is this any good?"

Once you ask that question, you are judging, and your creativity is sapped. You are converging in the middle of a divergent thinking session.

Let yourself generate/write/diverge with absolute love and delight.

Once you've written, you can go back and read with selection and perfection (convergence).

When people say, "there is no such thing as a bad idea," this is what they're referring to. Do not judge the ideas as they come. Give them shelter and welcome. Don't judge them (yet). Judge them in a separate editing/selecting session.

Table 3: *Divergence & Convergence*

| Divergence: Creating by Addition | Convergence: Creating by Subtraction |

Divergence is "yes and" – creating by addition. Convergence is poetry, sculpture, photography – creating by subtraction.

One last word on diverging and converging. They are the inhale and exhale of the creative process. We all do both. We usually like one over the other, value one over the other, identify as one vs. the other. But we must embrace both – and keep each in their place for best creative practice and outcomes. There is significant research that PROVES that originality/quality of ideas and quantity of creative output is improved simply by separating divergent and convergent thinking sessions.[viii]

Write without second-guessing yourself, and you'll be happier, in flow, leading to better writing. There's always time to hate everything you wrote later.

Brainstorming

Separating divergent and convergent thinking is the defining characteristic of brainstorming[ix] – invented in 1938 by Alex F. Osborn, a founder of BBD&O advertising agency. The concept revolutionized advertising creativity and has become a household word.

Be aware. People think of brainstorming only happening in a conference room with a big, rowdy bunch of people, pizza, nerf guns, colorful markers, and giant pads.

Brainstorming can be effective alone at your own desk, what defines brainstorming is simply the separation of the two kinds of thinking. And when you consciously do that, your creativity will improve.

The concept of separating one thinking session – ideating/writing – from the other – selecting/editing – helps us achieve our most original thinking by letting ideas and content flow unfettered. There's a time to edit, but not as you write.

Deliberate Creativity is the power to sit down, summon the "muse," and be at your best for the creativity at hand. Deliberate Creativity is also a graphic model that shows us how our brains work when we're creating. It is the best iteration of what's going on up there as you noodle through plots, characters, and fictional worlds (or any creative thinking, really).

Table 4: *Deliberate Creativity Thinking Model*

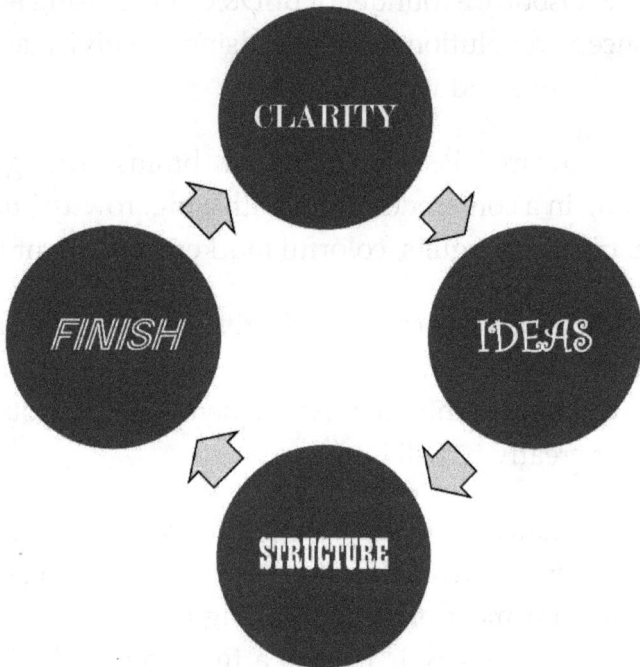

CLARITY

IDEAS

STRUCTURE

FINISH

Based on the Foursight Model of Creative Thinking[1]

A Little Creative Theory History

In 1954, Alex Osborne joined forces with Sydney Parnes in Buffalo State College, SUNY, New York, and developed the first creative thinking process model, called Creative Problem Solving (CPS), or the Osborne-Parnes model. It identified six thinking phases and activities.

1. MESS-FINDING / OBJECTIVE FINDING

2. FACT-FINDING

3. PROBLEM-FINDING

4. IDEA-FINDING

5. SOLUTION-FINDING

6. ACTION-FINDING

It can be a little complex for use in everyday life, and its language does not invite adoption. The Foursight Thinking Model, [x] simplified the process to four phases of thinking and one executive step – asking yourself questions to know where in the process to enter, based on where you are now.

Primarily, it reduced the process to four thinking phases, which made it easier to use and understand. It is the basis for Deliberate Creativity that we use to help us write with more ease and satisfaction.

Deliberate Creativity Today

What goes on when you're creating? This thinking model is an *observed* model. It tells us what is going on when creativity is working. It is not a "how-to," rather a "how-it-is" demonstration of a creative mind at work.

- First, you find CLARITY. You look at the big picture, sense gaps, identify opportunities and challenges, and get a direction.

- Next you get IDEAS. Your brain begins supplying solutions for some of the challenges and has ideas about options that arose in the clarifying stage.

- Then, you select and perfect. You begin to add STRUCTURE to your ideas and develop something. A song, a scene, a book, a comedy routine, a movie, a poem.

- Lastly, you FINISH it. You finish the work, the phase you're in, the thought. You put it in the world or make the plan to take these steps.

This graphic models how you think as an arc for your whole project, but also how your brain cycles through thoughts to do something small, like name a character or think of a word that rhymes with "Bob."

You run through this cycle quickly and repetitively as you create, and all the many turns around the cycle also add up to one grand arc of how you create the whole project.

Your creative thinking runs in this cycle – Clarity – Ideas – Structure – Finish – as predictably and routinely as a washing machine cycles through wash, rinse, and spin.

This is what naturally happens. And since we know how it works, we can also use this as the map for how to get back on track, when somehow, you've lost your creativity. This is the map to get back to it.

You just have to ask:

- What phase of the cycle were you in when you got stuck?

- What would naturally come next?

- Why did I falter?

    o Is it because I dislike the phase of thinking I was in?

    o Or because I dread the next phase of thinking?

    o Is it because I love the phase of thinking I'm in, and don't want to progress to a less comfortable phase/way of thinking?

- What is my relationship to the next phase of thinking?

Nope... I can feel you checking out.

Maybe this feels a little dry or boring – certainly not magical. You might be asking, "What does any of this have to do with writing?"

Writers get lost sometimes. We all need a map, occasionally.

The magic comes from learning about how YOU think creatively in relation to this model.

- What do you do especially well?

- What do you like?

- What do you avoid doing?

- How does this love/hate relationship cause your writer's block/stuck/stall/fight?

Write, Without the Fight

This is the foundation of Write Without the Fight FB group, and the Write Without the Fight Challenge. This information can redefine your fights and fits within your creative process. Getting cozy with this map is your best way to diagnose your thinking profile and figure out which creativity hack can make your writing life a lot easier!

Let's find the correlation between your thinking style and the creative process so you can predict and prevent your doubts and delay. Ready for more science? YAY!!

CHERYL CLARK, FORMER SPANISH TEACHER, AND SCHOOL LIBRARIAN ...

"When I started with Julia, I felt like I needed some sort of outside force to compel me to sit down and write. I worked hard and wrote over 10,000 words! I hope to finish my novel, find a literary agent, and get published."

NAME YOUR CREATIVE THINKING STYLE

- *Don't Panic*
- *What's Your Creative Superpower?*
- *What's Your Creative Achilles Heel?*
- *How Can You Predict and Prevent the Struggle?*

Don't Panic

You've just learned there's a name for your creative strength. Yeah, yeah, you knew that about yourself. What's the big deal? I obviously knew I was a strong ideator – I'd been a professional brainstormer for decades. It was nice to be validated and defined, but that part wasn't news to me.

You've also just seen your creative struggle. That's where people might panic. Your ego does not like to come face to face with weakness. Denial, anger and forgetfulness kick in right away.

Don't let it. Own your strength, yes. But own your struggle too. It's yours to master, delegate, barter or collaborate. It's already been defining you for years, by keeping you cramped and scared. Now, instead, it can just be an acceptable part of how you create. You lose energy in a certain phase of the creative process.

What you do with that information is what can make you a creative superhero.

What's Your Creative Superpower?

Okay, let's refocus on the four phases of creative thinking. There are four ways of thinking that progress in order, whirring in your brain, quickly and slowly in service of your creativity.

Most of us have at least one thinking skill we gain energy from. And because it gives us energy, for the most part, we love and excel at it. It's fun for us! (I mean, who doesn't like energy?) Do you know which is your best strength?

Table 5: *The Phases of Deliberate Creativity*

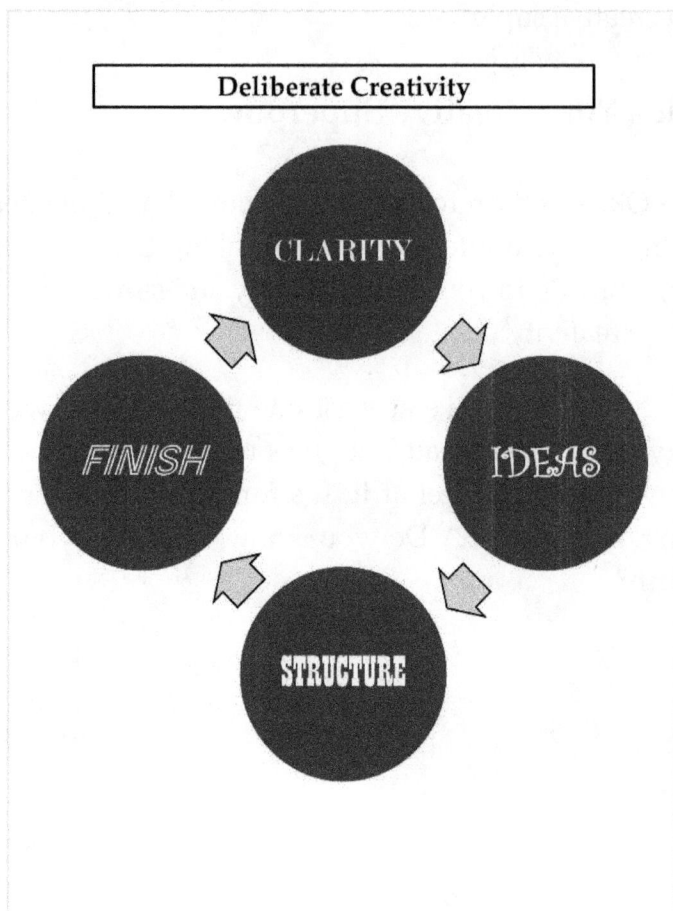

Each phase gives us an outcome, generated by that phase of creativity –

Clarity	Identify challenges and options
Ideas	Come up with original and exciting ideas
Structure	Develop the best ideas into their form – scene, book, poem, script
Finish	Create and implement the plan to make ideas reality

Each phase has its lovers and haters.

TRY IT

Can you guess which is your creative superpower? (Hint: It could be more than one.) Here's a little more to go on.

Which phase(s) do you love to do? Where do you thrive? Is there another phase at which you excel?

I excel at _____ (and _____).

Table 6: *What Kind of Creative Thinker are You?*

If you crave	Then you focus on...
Clarity	SEEING THE BIG PICTURE
Ideas	GETTING THE BIG IDEA
Structure	GETTING IT PERFECT
The Finish line	GETTING IT DONE

What's Your Creative Achilles Heel?

Do you know the Greek myth of Achilles? At birth, it was prophesied that Achilles would die a young man. His mother, the goddess Thetis, took her son to the River Styx in Hades, and dipped him head first into the running water, to gain the power of invulnerability. Her hand held him fast by thumb and forefinger on his heel – which therefore did not get the desired protection. Achilles grew up to be a legendary warrior. He was thought to be invincible but ultimately, was killed by an arrow in the heel. So, the metaphor is used to imply great strength with an unknown, or unseen vulnerability.

4Ancient art, Achilles, public domain

The arrow hit its target – the Achilles heel. Consider how much stronger Achilles might have been if he'd known about his vulnerability. Or might he have lived in fear of the chance it gave others to attack or criticize him?

What's your Achilles heel? And how will you treat it in your life?

As we said, there are FOUR phases of creative thinking. They are all *required* to take a creative concept – large or small – to completion. You can't just skip or skimp one phase and hope to succeed.

You could manage to skate through a weak spot now and then, due to specific circumstances – like unexpected help from a differently abled creative thinker. Next time you want to replicate that success, you might not be so lucky. You could come up against what people vaguely call "writer's block."

You could be stuck. And stuck sucks. It hurts. It makes you question the basics, like your self-worth.

There is likely a phase of creative thinking that stymies you. (If you're lucky it is just one.) You are highly likely to be blind to it. Your precious, petty ego won't let you see or acknowledge it. That same overactive ego is working overtime to discredit that way of thinking and dislike it in other people, too.

Unaware, you are a mess. Perhaps talented, perhaps hardworking, but doomed, nonetheless. You need to be aware of your own Achilles heel.

Come to the WWTF Facebook Group and let us know what creative thinking profile you believe are.

I am strong with _____.

I struggle with _____.

My Story: I didn't realize I was blocked.

I just thought I had too many ideas. I didn't really think there was a "fix" for that. In fact, I loved having too many ideas. It made me resourceful, flexible, and of course, valuable in a brainstorming session.

At work, I was a professional brainstormer for major companies like Nickelodeon, Warner Bros., Heinz Ketchup, HBO, and others. Anyone who knew me knew I was an above-average ideator.

But in my own creative endeavors, I *repeatedly* failed to clarify, so I got started on a new idea and a month or so later, something went a little wrong. And since ideas were plentiful, it was easier for me to jump to a new idea instead of stopping to clarify the problem and come up with solutions. I was blocked in the busiest way. I was talented, crazy creative, and not performing in a satisfying way. I wasted years not realizing I was stuck in this pattern. Even if I got a hint at the problem, I didn't think about — and didn't seek — a solution.

But I wasn't writing or finishing anything of my own. I wasn't *doing* anything, it felt like.

JULIA'S STORY

I had a GREAT IDEA.	I got started RIGHT AWAY.	Something went a LITTLE WRONG.	Oh, well. I'll get a NEW IDEA!
I had a NEW IDEA.	I got started RIGHT AWAY	Something went a LITTLE WRONG.	Oh, well. I'll get a NEW IDEA!

5 *4 Clients & a Funeral*, Julia Roberts

I got fed up and started seeking help! Note: People, friends, other writers, or your mother are not always helpful. This is what people who loved me said…

Help that's not helpful (I've heard it all.)

~ Just pick one idea and stick with it

~ You have to f-o-c-u-s

~ Quit trying to do your "crazy" ideas

~ You're just a flibberty-gibbet (a flake, a free spirit) and always will be

~Just do the work. You can't be allergic to the work

It's like "duh!" and "shut up!" at the same time. I would do those things if I could, if they were in my creative nature. Too many ideas was my obvious Achilles Heel.

Professional Help

Just as my first book was coming out, I felt paralyzed. I sought life coaching and ultimately trained as a coach with Dr. Martha Beck, author, life coach, and columnist for *O Magazine*, and Oprah Book of the Month Club author! I finally quieted those pesky, belittling thoughts.

I found PEACE (between my ears)

Still, I was not "there" yet. I found Eric Maisel, PhD, author of 20 plus books on creativity. Dr. Maisel conceived the idea of a creativity coach, and so I trained with him as a creativity coach. He has helped any number of creative people from all sorts of disciplines continue creating, even when they thought all was lost. I wanted to do that for writers.

I found PURPOSE (and my PEOPLE)

Lastly, I got my Masters in Creativity from Buffalo State College, the premiere degree-granting institution in

Creative Studies. I learned about my creative thinking profile and tools to help me through my weak spots and allow me to perform at my top level and finish my work.

I found POWER

And I began to share it with writers.

Get help! Who's on your helping team? And are they helpful? Some might commiserate, but can they give you material help with your creative nature? Your creative process?

Achilles wasn't aware of his vulnerable spot until it killed him. Your creative struggle is not likely to kill you, but it may be killing your ideas, your creative dreams, and your options. It is sapping you of your power.

How can you predict and prevent the struggle?

- Are you able to see your best creative thinking phase(s)?

- Can you see the one (or more) phase(s) of creativity that cause(s) you to struggle?

6 https://www.wikiwand.com/en/Samburu_National_Reserve

If you'd like certainty, or a more detailed view, check out the Creative Selfie – three professional creativity assessments.

I've assembled three professional creativity tests to give you a thorough, 360-degree view of how you create what's unique about your thinking skills and struggles, and what you can do to claim your greatest creative position in this world. [xi]

Read more about the Creative Selfie:
https://go.decodingcreativity.com/creative-selfie

> ### *Debra Galant, Award-winning podcaster, painter, novelist, and former NY Times Columnist...*
>
> Is a successful writer, by any measure.
>
> What could she get out of the Creative Selfie? She was dying to know. Here's what she said: "I learned I was putting more restrictions on myself than I realized. I was not pushing the rules in my creativity. In the next several weeks, I found myself pushing the rules more than before, just in my life. "
>
> "I started to have a sense that life was more malleable, and these barriers weren't necessarily there. That was a really powerful result of that test."

When is a Cup Not Just a Cup?

For the first 40ish years of my life, as I mentioned, I tried to skip clarifying – an important part of the creative process.

As soon as I was tested and saw my incredibly low score in clarifying there was no more denying it. What was interesting was that for the next several days, I started to see that both my husband and my mother were clarifiers.

7 "Numbered Cups" by srqpix,license,CC BY 2.0

I was at my mom's, and I asked her to hand me a cup. She said: "Do you want a small cup? I have this large one? Is it for a cold drink? Or are you having coffee? Oo, how about this new one? Do you like that?"

So many questions! She was clarifying.

I was crazy impatient! I rolled my eyes...

"OMG, Mom, I've changed my mind!

Do you have a gun?"

All around me, people were clarifying, and I was resisting and judging their help.

I know my weak spot now. And it cannot taunt me.

Until the assessment, I didn't realize that I avoided clarifying. And even if I'd had an insight about that, I'm sure I wouldn't have cared.

Clarifiers drove me crazy, without my realizing it. Why? Because they reminded my fragile little ego what I was bad at. And clarifiers like to focus the creative conversation on the part of the process where I was uncomfortable.

If you are dreading someone or something or rolling your eyes about someone's creative contribution or comment, you are probably in denial about your own creative shortcoming. Your ego is working overtime to keep your dear, fragile self from seeing the truth about your creativity.

Do you have a "cup" skulking in your closet?

If, like me, you know there is a part of the process that routinely trips you up, then you can be prepared for it, right? It won't mess with your sense of self-worth or make you worry you'll never finish this thing. You're not calling your sister and complaining, or eating ice cream in front of the TV. You're not forever starting and abandoning creative projects when they get a little weird or tough.

You learn a hack. (And there are lots of them!)

We've got a bunch of them coming up in The Don't-Get-Stopped-In-Your-Tracks Hacks section. Each of them is useful for anyone. But your hack is a lifesaver. Yours helps you prevent failure and meltdown.

In the Decoding Creativity blog and in the free FB group, we share a lot of hacks, and remind each other to use them. This is why a group can be a big help to writers – even though writing is a solitary sport. (Read the blog @decodingcreativity.com/blog)

Have You Ever Sung in a Chorus?

It is much easier to sing in unison, right? You are emboldened by all the soprano, alto, tenor, and bass voices that surround you. You're just singing your part. Being part of the Mighty Writers group is like singing in a chorus. Your voice is strong and clear, as if others were singing alongside you. But then, of course, yours is the only voice that shows up on the page.

8 Public Domain, CC licensed use

NAME IT - RECAP

- A disease with no name cannot be understood, and therefore it is hard for it to be fixed or cured.

- You think as everyone else does when creating. What is unique to you is what strengths and struggles you bring to each phase of creating. First you seek:

  1. Clarity, then

  2. Ideas, then

  3. Structure, and finally,

  4. Finish

- Can you name your strength within that process?

- Can you pinpoint where you fall into dread, lose energy, skip or skimp a phase?

- Can you see how this natural ability – and denial of struggle – has shaped your creative endeavors?

HELLO, FRIEND. HELLO, FRIEND. THAT'S LAME. MAYBE I SHOULD GIVE YOU A NAME. BUT THAT'S A SLIPPERY SLOPE. YOU'RE ONLY IN MY HEAD. WE HAVE TO REMEMBER THAT.

~ROBERT ALDERSON, MR. ROBOT

3RD STEP – CLAIM IT

9 Apollo Landing, Wikimedia, Public domain, Creative Commons license

CLAIM YOUR CREATIVE STRENGTHS AS YOUR OWN

- *Honor How You Create and Think*
- *Skip the Dread*
- *Get Out of Your Head*
- *Enjoy Writing Again*
- *Claim Your Strength*

Honor How You Create and Think

10 The-Death-of-Munrow_CC0 1.0

Our survival instincts keep us from believing we're good enough. Our entire being believes that in order to stay alive, we must continuously compare ourselves to others. (Operating note: You don't have to outrun a tiger. You just have to outrun the next guy. You are *driven* to compare your speed, wits, and ingenuity to his.) Humans are hardwired to compare as part of our survival instinct. It is hard to work around. And yet, constant comparisons can ding your ego and get you stuck "up in your head." Doubt and delays are inevitable.

People are four times more likely to see how we are deficient than to see how we are superlative.

It takes a conscious and courageous effort to get past survival programming, but it must be done. Start by seeing your own glory, magnified times four, to overcome the baked-in bias we all have. Remember, we are 4x more likely to see our failings vs our triumphs. At first, seeing your triumph 4x, in 4 ways, may feel braggy, and your inner critic will push back. But based on our instinct to diminish what good we see in ourselves, a four times upgrade might just bring your perception closer to reality.

Instead of comparing your abilities with someone else's, glory in your own. Honor your strong suit and don't apologize for your foibles. Use a tool or a collaborator to bolster your struggle spots – and write.

Your way of thinking creatively is not simply good enough – it is astounding.

Skip the Dread

What do you dread about creating? What happens over and over till you fear you can't take it anymore?

_____.

Mighty Writers tell me:

- "I write for 30-35,000 words and then... nothing."

- "I can't start. That first sentence has to be perfect."

- "I can't find the time, and every night I go to bed feeling like a fraud. I'm not a writer."

- "I fear someone – anyone – will tell me this isn't good enough."

- "I don't have original enough ideas."

- "By now, I can't even free-write."

We don't all have to be Shakespeare, Charles Dickens, or Jane Austen. (Remember, we just have to outrun the next guy.) We have to take what natural talents and insights we were given and shape them into the ideas, stories, and missives that we are called to write.

83

To do that, we have to be able to act in faith. We have to silence the dread. And we have to believe this time will be different. But how?

Right now, you probably have a "dreadful" understanding of things you can't do, or don't do well. It's like the feeling you have about a weird stomachache or an unexplained lump on your leg or head.

Here's how it goes: you dread the truth. You're afraid to ask – it might be worse than you can even imagine. You would rather hide and worry than act.

Alternately, you can't take it anymore. You want the truth… even if the truth is you can't write for beans, and you might as well give up now.

But somehow, you still can't bring yourself to ask for help. It would make it final, real. You sink into dread.

We all have lumps, aches, and suspicious moles in our creative processes, too. And it's not like we don't notice them. We've written ourselves into painful corners before. But the thoughts and feelings that keep us up at night can be diagnosed, cured or mitigated. We can get back to writing *without the dread*.

There is real help. And it is science.

Scientists have been working on the issue of what inhibits and/or enhances creativity for about 70 years. (We've seen your "mole," and "lumps like that." We've felt that "ache" before. We have remedies.)

There are two important tasks: name your creative thinking style (check) and claim it. It can feel like arrogance, but lay claim to what is special in you. It is not everyone, but it *is* you. It is also time to look at what ails you and be okay with it. Once you know, you know.

If he'd known, Achilles could have worn taller boots.

The real value in seeing it is, you're no longer trying to not see it. You're not pretending to yourself or others that it's not a struggle. You're not hoping no one else notices this appalling failing in you.

It's yours. You're working with it. You got this.

It is time to find a cure for that Achilles heel of yours so you don't have to worry about it anymore. Yeah, it might flair up again, and you might need to take it slow sometimes, but it won't take you down next time.

There's a hack for that.

Barbra Cosentino, psychotherapist, freelance writer...

had her first poem, "My Grandmother's Trunk", published in *Chubby Girl Magazine*. Since then, she's written for the *New York Times*, *Next Avenue, Medscape*, and many other publications.

"When I began with Julia, I feared that I might never write again. After my workdays, I watched Netflix, nibbled on junk food and assiduously avoided anything to do with writing.

"Working with Julia, I filled two big notebooks with free associative writing, having met my goal of enjoying the process without worrying about a product. With no conscious effort, I think the amorphous ideas I've had for a memoir are beginning to take shape. I hope to eat less chocolate and to write many, many more words!"

Get Out of Your Head

Oh, those pesky thoughts.

We writers think the brain is everything, that our thoughts are our only coin. And it's true. We do our thing cerebrally.

But absolute power corrupts absolutely.

As soon as you give your brain unchecked power, it will take advantage. It will run you through hoops, own your day, clench your stomach, race your heart, make your breath shallow and panicked. Your head is not always nice. Sometimes you gotta get outta there.

How do you get out of your head?

It is a matter of check and balance. Bring your body into the mix.

Your brain lives in your head, yes, but also in your heart and stomach.

There is actual brain matter – neurons – that extend from the brain in your skull to the offsite brain functions established in your heart and stomach.

This has long been intuited in phrases such as "follow your heart," and take a "gut check."

As a brain-lover myself, I resisted this new science. I thought I knew my brain, that it was reliable, smart, and logical. And thinking with your heart or your gut was just… suspect. In fact, until I had a baby, I pretty much thought my body existed to walk my brain around.

But new research has established a direct and sometimes inter-regulatory relationship between the three brain sites: head, heart and gut. And one of the time-honored, effective ways to get out of your head is to get into your body. Switch gears. Honor your other brain sites.

Here's what happens. OFTEN. Your head-brain is causing distress with an ego story.

- "This is never going to work."

- "Is this any good?"

- "Who do you think you are?"

- "You never finish anything anyway..."

Author's Note: I just had the thought, "This should be done by now," And my heart sank. Before I even noticed the thought, I had pushed back from my desk and was eating a cookie.

Cognition – Thinking about Thinking

We believe the story. We rarely question it. Like at all. So, the brain acts accordingly and releases the appropriate hormones and chemicals.

Next thing you know, you *feel* the thought. Your body slumps or your jaw clenches. Maybe your stomach tightens. Maybe there's a pain between the shoulder blades. And now you believe that story even more, because the brains in your heart and gut are reinforcing it. The feelings and the story match.

You feel bad, and now you've stopped writing. You're shut down by a pesky thought that may or may not be true. But you suddenly don't care about the thought. It's gone.

Like a drive-by shooter, a negative thought releases hormones and chemicals into your body, and moves on. It *triggers* feelings you weren't having a minute earlier.

Now you're sinking, and new thoughts come to mind, and you're all, "Nothing I do ever makes a difference anyway, so why bother?"

STOP THAT THOUGHT BEFORE IT STOPS YOU.

Perhaps you didn't notice the first thought, and you're quickly down in the dumps. Or right now, you're feeling pretty great. But you've had those pesky thoughts before, right? What self-judging thought do you have? Any "stopping thought" will do.

TRY IT

Quick. Write it down. Literally. Get that slippery, icky thought onto paper. Now look at it.

The thought I just had about my work was:

_____.

Write it down, before you lose it!

Is it true?

Ask yourself, *Is it true?* Work along with me, as I take my thought from above, and answer the four questions, and do the turnaround (below).

"I should be done with this book by now."

Ugh. Is it true?

This inquiry into the truth of your painful thoughts is the brilliant work of Byron Katie, author of *Loving What Is*[xii]. It consists of four questions. (For deeper guidance in this practice, see: thework.com, and my blog post on the topic: Disciplined Thinking)

1. Is it true?

2. Can you absolutely know it's true?

3. How do you feel when you think the thought?

4. Who would you be without that thought?

Then you do a turnaround.

- What is an opposite thought that might be just as true or truer?

- Can you believe that new thought?

- Find three proofs from your life to prove the new and opposite thought.

- How does the new thought make you feel?

So, addressing the painful thought, I answer these questions. (You do it with your thought.)

"I should be done with this by now."

1. Is it true?

Unexamined, it feels true. Like, yeah, I'm the slowest, laziest writer in existence. And/or – I'm so bad at guesstimating my time. How stupid am I to think this would only take...

(Notice: I just started in on a new painful thought i.e., *I'm so bad at guesstimating my time. How stupid am I to think this would only take...*) This is why you need to do this in writing. Before long, you'll have one or more new painful thoughts that support the first thought, and you're down a rabbit hole. Instead... stay with the thought and this process.

2. Can you absolutely know it's true?

Should I BE done? Well, I'm not, so how can it be "absolutely" true that I should be? In what universe should I be able to transmute time, creativity, and productivity to make this myth true?

3. How do you feel when you think the thought?

Okay, it is not true. And yet, unexamined, that thought made me feel bad, made me push back from my desk, might have caused unhealthy eating and worst of all – derailed my writing! The drive-by shooter hit its mark.

My brain "thunk" and my mood sunk.

4. Who would you be without that thought?

This is heavy, deep, and real (as we used to say in the Seventies.) Who could I be if I never entertained the thought "this should be done by now?" If I simply let things take the time they took and enjoyed the process?* Who is that person? And what might she be capable of writing? OMG.

*And BTW, it's going to take the time it takes whether or not I "let" it.

The Turnaround

Do I have three proofs from my life that say this thought isn't true? I can prove it's NOT true,

1. It is as it is. I am about 50% done. Therefore, that is what "should" be.

2. I've been working hard since I started writing. Therefore, I couldn't have just ramped it up enough to more than double my output.

3. I know that "shoulds" are often suspect thoughts I use to punish myself, and this was just one of those "should-y" thoughts.

The new thought, "I *shouldn't* be done by now." Or "I am right where I should be," feels relaxed and reassuring.

I will choose to believe this new thought. "I'm right where I should be." The second, third, and 100th time I have the other thought, I remind myself, "I'm right where I should be," and I will again choose to believe the new thought.

I've proven it to myself. I know I'm where I belong. I can just block that old disproven thought (and its associated, bad, false feelings).

Result: I stay at my desk. I maintain my mood and productivity. I'm bullet proof. (Until I have a new painful thought. And then I repeat the process.)

Try It

When I first learned of Katie's turnaround method, I carried a notebook and scribbled down hundreds of negative thoughts, as they happened. When I had time, I examined them in the manner above, and it was life-altering. My beliefs shifted as I replaced damaging thoughts. Beliefs are just thoughts you've thought 10,000 times. They can and do shift as the underlying thoughts get disproven and replaced.

I WENT YEARS NOT FINISHING ANYTHING. BECAUSE OF COURSE, WHEN YOU FINISH SOMETHING, YOU CAN BE JUDGED.

~ERICA JONG

Enjoy Writing Again

Writing should feel good. Good writing comes from states of flow, and flow has been described as an *orgasm for the brain*. We temporarily lose track of everything else – our bodies, our surroundings. We are in the zone, and it is good. Don't let yourself get overwhelmed. Anne Lamott, author of *Bird by Bird*[xiii], talks of the 1" square frame she keeps on her desk. It reminds her that she only has to write what you might see through that 1" frame.

11"Hungry Mother Picture Frame" by vastateparksstaff _ CC BY 2.0

.You're not writing a novel or a movie. Right now, you're just writing the one sentence, the one paragraph, the one scene where something happens.

And that one scene needs all your love and attention right now. It doesn't need half your brain to be beating itself up about how much there is left to do.

Bill Kenower, author of *Fearless Writing* [xiv], brings back the joy in two simple and brilliant ways.

1. As he says, remember what flow feels like. Before you try to write, take the ordeal out of it. Don't gird your loins, set a timer, or place an Elf on the Shelf to supervise yourself. Just sit a minute and remember what flow feels like. Your brain will want back in.

2. Close your eyes and ask your brain: "Show me." Let your dear brain play the movie in your head of what is about to happen in your writing. Your imagination will pre-write the scene, and you'll just be capturing it all. Have you ever had the feeling that someone else was writing for you? (See my blog post, How Not to Think Bad @decodingcreativity.com/how-not-to-think-bad)

Claim Your Strength as Your Own

It is time to understand that what you are is special, unique to you, and needed in the world. What you aren't can be fixed, helped, and lived with. But there is no need to apologize for it. You don't have to hide it or feel threatened by people who excel in that particular skill. You are not flawed. You are uniquely abled, and what you offer is amazing.

You are secure in your strengths, and open to help and collaboration where you need it. You're going to make your visions real, as you claim – AND WIELD – your creative abilities.

Next up, we're going to figure out how.

CLAIM IT - RECAP

- We are big-headed and craven at the same time.

- Honor how you think – strength and struggle.

- Achilles could have worn taller boots, had he known his weak spot.

- Your "Tall Boots" options include

    o Better, honest, information about yourself and your creativity

    o Creativity tools

    o Better collaboration

    o Delegation

    o Barter and more

- There is no shame in knowing your weak spot. It liberates you from apologizing, obfuscating and worrying that someone will see yours.

- When you have a painful or stopping thought – write it down. And check its truthfulness, before you let it sink your mood and defeat your dreams.

- And now, you've come to a healthy understanding of your abilities, enjoy your writing again. It helps to remember, it can be fun.

Sutapa Das, writer...

was stuck in her writing and wasn't sure how to get unstuck. "Julia helped me gain a better understanding of my creative process and gave me a set of tools to turn to when I feel lost and directionless. Seeing the ways my brain works, I now have renewed appreciation for the importance of self-kindness and strive to maintain a safe and non-judgmental inner environment for my creativity and a habit of making space and time for my writing in the middle of an otherwise hectic day."

4TH STEP – TAME IT

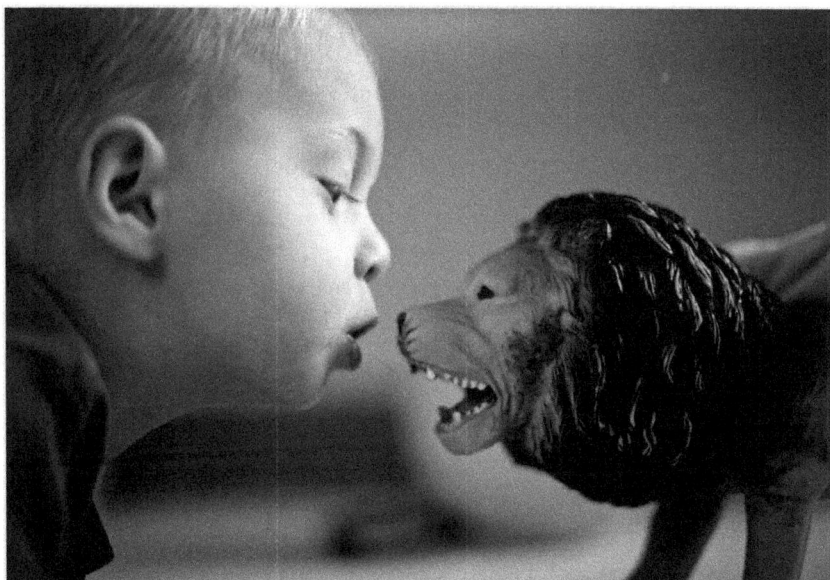

12 Flickr, CC licensed use

Tame it – Proven Tools to Write Right Through Your Weak Spots

- *Why Bother?*
- *Don't-Get-Stopped-in-Your-Tracks Hacks*
  - What You Have To Do
  - Why Can't I Get Started?
  - My Ideas are No Good
  - I Write 30,000 Words and Then I Quit/Get Stuck
  - I Never Finish Anything
- *H2 Keep Writing and Feel Good*

YOU MUST STAY DRUNK ON WRITING,
SO REALITY CANNOT DESTROY YOU.

~ RAY BRADBURY

Why Bother?

Why bother? There is more than one answer to this painful question. Many of us just don't let ourselves write. We do other "important" tasks – like making money, making dinner, or making do with the unexamined life we've relegated ourselves to.

"Is it worth it?" is a question we ask ourselves. And we feel smart to be "managing our time" and "prioritizing adulting." We think we're smart to gauge whether this is time well-spent.

Why bother? Is it worth it? Writers often question if it is even worth the time and the work to write. This is a toughie. My clients – Mighty Writers like you – tell me this is one of their biggest reasons to delay or even quit writing. It is hard to tell if it's "worth it."

What creates "worth" in your life?

- Of course, there's monetary worth. And it is always hard to predict if your writing will generate money unless you write things that are needed by businesses and other organizations - proposals, instruction booklets, marketing and advertising copy

  o When Elizabeth Gilbert asked her memoir "characters" for the rights to use their names and stories, for *Eat, Pray, Love,* she told them, "Don't worry, no one reads my books."

  o Whether or not your book will make money is hard to predict.

  o And yet it will be you who drives the creativity of your marketing and determines its monetary value in your life.

- There's also emotional worth. Is it worth the *sturm* and *drang* – the emotional roller coaster ride – begun by trying to write something that is important to you? This equation can be significantly changed by defanging the guilt and shame people feel when they get overwhelmed or quit "for no reason."

- *"MARKETING IS NOT WHAT LURES A WRITER TO THIS PURSUIT. MARKETING IS THE ADVERSARY THAT ARRIVES SMUGGLED INSIDE THE TROJAN HORSE OF ONE'S CREATIVE IMPULSE."*

  ~ JANE FRIEDMAN

- Is it worth it physically? This calculation may be about time in a chair at a computer. But the more important calculation, in my mind, are the other behaviors we use to mask and suppress our callings.

We eat, drink, drug, shop, speed, and fight with our loved ones. Is it worth it to you to get that drama on the page, instead of keeping drama in your life?

- And there is spiritual worth. Is it worth doing? Is it right to do it? Is it mine to do?

  o Do you deserve writing time? Yes. You're worth it.

o If you truly want to write, it means you likely have something to share with the world. We deserve the benefit of your ideas and insights.

WRITING IS ITS OWN REWARD

~ HENRY MILLER

It is time to recalculate worth. Write with more ease and satisfaction and you'll write at your best. You're more likely to achieve exceptional – saleable – writing. But you'll also be writing for yourself. You will follow your own nose, in the direction you want to explore, and write what is most interesting to you. You won't be writing "uphill."

If you love it, it will show, and others will follow you there. Let's make writing fun again.

An artist needs to be allowed to waste time. In reality, nothing is wasted. It all becomes your thoughts, insights, and writing. Writing can be like painting or playing guitar. You can do it for yourself. You can do it in hopes of being published. But you can let yourself write, even if you can't yet see its monetary value in your life. It doesn't have to be "worth it" to be worthwhile.

The Don't-Get-Stopped-In-Your-Tracks Hacks

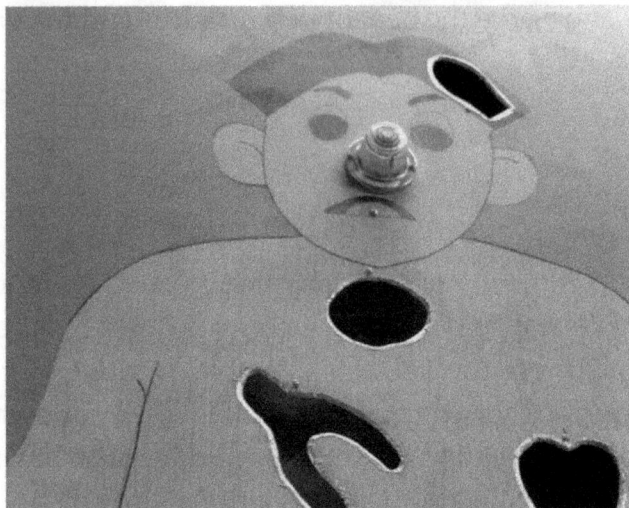

13 Operation board game is TM Hasbro Games. Photo: Pixabay

Zonk! You make a little mistake, and you're stopped in your tracks. But hold on a minute. It does not have to be that way.

Find your hack. Write your work. Put it in the world. With the right hack, you can do your important work without getting zonked.

I call these "hacks" to be cool, tbh. In actuality, these are tested, researched tools that have been impactful for tens of thousands of willing subjects. These "hacks" are based in a deep understanding of how the brain works when it's creating. Heady stuff.

It's like aspirin. You don't need to understand how it was invented, or even how it works in your body. You just know that it gets rid of headaches.

When you Write Without the Fight, that's exactly what you get, headache/writing relief. Magically. Through science. You don't need a degree in Creative Studies. You've got me.

I CAN SHAKE OFF EVERYTHING AS I WRITE; MY SORROWS DISAPPEAR, MY COURAGE IS REBORN.

~ ANNE FRANK

What You Have to Do

You know what you have to do. You have a list as long as your arm.

Mighty Hack[xv]

To get started, clarify your challenges. What is keeping you from writing? What goes through your mind?

"I have to write that chapter."

"I have to get back to that script."

"I swear, I'll start first thing tomorrow morning."

Retool how you talk to yourself. Use "might." "Might" is a word that is very powerful in our brains. We are powerless over the word "might," our curiosity is perked up. "Might" implies opportunity or threat, so our survival instinct is pricked.

Reword the challenge:

- How might I write that chapter?

- How might I get back to that script?

- How might I get this started tomorrow morning?

TRY IT

Say one of the sentences from the first bullet cluster that is relevant to you.

I have to write…

Notice how the sentence makes you feel. Where do you feel it?

Now, close your eyes and say/think the analogous sentence from the second bullet cluster. How does that feel different?

How might I write…

By using the word "might" we begin to seek solutions instantaneously, instead of mounting resistance.

How might I...?

What might be all the ways to...?

We have upshifted. Our locus of thinking shifts. Remember, Table 1, *The Triune Brain?* We've shifted from the lizard brain to the story brain.

When you're thinking "I have to..." you are typically thinking with your lizard brain, which operates from fear. Using "might" upshifts your thinking to the neo-cortex/story brain. This engages your imagination to solve your problems and come up with new ideas, new ways forward.

Doesn't it feel instantly better? The tool is simple and mighty and elemental to Deliberate Creativity.

Why Can't I Get Started?

Clarifying is not my best skillset. As I said, I'm sort of obstructive of clarifying, actually. Why? Because I like getting and sharing ideas. But to be *useful* ideas, clarity must come first. And it is agonizingly slow and keeps me out of the heaven that is shooting the shit and throwing out ideas that make me happy. If I'm in a room full of people, it makes them happy, too. I'm showing my value, and it's easy for me.

If someone in that same room is clarifying – asking questions like Why? and What's stopping you? – over and over and over again, I start to feel stupid. I might even start to worry that I look stupid. Clarifying can make me anxious – or it used to. And we all know that a confused mind shuts down.

I've done my level best to avoid clarifying for much of my adult life by working as a brainstormer. Things were supposed to be clarified before I got there and decided after I left. It was a good gig. Every conference room I entered had candy or pizza and post-it notes and colored pens. I'd spew ideas and make money. Great gig.

But when I'm working on my own stuff, in my own office, no one clarifies for me. That felt liberating at first. Woohoo! I can work on my most exciting idea! And GO! But a couple of months later, I'd see a glitch. Something wasn't working. I'd have to stop. Bummer. It was such a great idea, I thought. Or was it? I never fully clarified what it might have been a great idea for, but obviously (at least, now, it's obvious) not for this situation.

After years of start and stop, wasting time and jumping to new ideas, I started to seek CLARITY. I pulled on my big girl pants and did the work

It took me years to come to the realization that I had a big blindspot, and a bigger attitude problem, about one part of the creative process.

The Why, What's Stopping You? Tool[xvi]

When it became *painful* and *painfully* OBVIOUS, I needed to value CLARITY, I used this tool – sometimes called the Ladder of Abstraction or Why, What's Stopping You. It helps you get to the bottom of what challenges you will face to achieve a goal, and how to clarify which ideas will work best in the circumstances.

Start with the goal statement. What are you trying to achieve? This could be a big goal, like having a bestseller, or a small goal, like making a scene work. Phrase your goal using the language, "It would be great if…"

It would be great if… this scene didn't feel wooden and sucky.

That's how goals start out. The language is negative and painful. Try it again a few more times. And try to get specific. Figure out what you're really trying to achieve.

IWBGI… this scene could show us how much mother and daughter care for each other, even if it's uncomfortable for them to say it.

Okay, stop here for a minute, and write your goal statements. Don't stop at one – or even two – write it a few ways. When it feels like something you actually want, you're ready to ask the questions, Why? and What's Stopping You?

Why? Why? Why?

I'm going to go forward with the example: "IWBGI I could show that they care for each other" as our current goal. And hopefully, you've stopped and arrived at a goal that matters to you – something with a tug for you.

WHY do you want that? Think about your answer.

And don't stop there – ask yourself for two other reasons WHY you want that. And then you continue to abstract your answers by asking WHY ELSE? six more times. (See below.) This exercise can bring you real clarity in your big WHY – the aspirations of what you're trying to achieve. (There's a blog post: Why, What's Stopping You? @ https://www.decodingcreativity.com/why-whats-stopping-you/)

Our example: "IWBGI I could show the mother and daughter care for each other"

- WHY is that important? The answers WHY could be about:

    1. upcoming scenes

2. clarifying the daughter's motivation

3. or proving the mother isn't as mean or heartless as she's about to seem

- (Just pulling reasons out of a hat, but you get the idea.)

- WHY ELSE? is an abstraction, from each vague answer

    1. Re: "Upcoming scenes," I might get more specific, like "the slap in Chapter Two will be more shocking."

    2. Re: "Daughter's motivation," I might abstract: "we need to see her conflict with her mother."

    3. An abstraction of "Proving the mother is not heartless" could be "the reader needs to be able to relate to mother."

As you go up the ladder of abstraction, you'll get deeper and more abstract as to your hopes and aspirations for the scene that is currently keeping you stuck.

Time to ask the second CLARITY question: *What's Stopping You?*

Here again, you're trying to get at what the problem is, by asking *WHAT'S STOPPING YOU?* nine times. If you answer this honestly, you can see what's holding you back from getting what you want. And from there you just have to decide whether those things are worth changing.

Examples of WHAT'S STOPPING YOU answers, could be specific to what you're trying to write and gain CLARITY ON – your niggling objections, like:

- "it doesn't make sense in this scene."

- "I don't know how to show the muted emotions."

- "I've written it three times and it's no good."

Continue to abstract your feelings and objections by asking WHAT ELSE? Two more times per column. (See the worksheet below.) Here's the exercise. You can print it out and use it to clarify your own dreams, big or small.

Table 7: *Why? What's Stopping You? Tool*

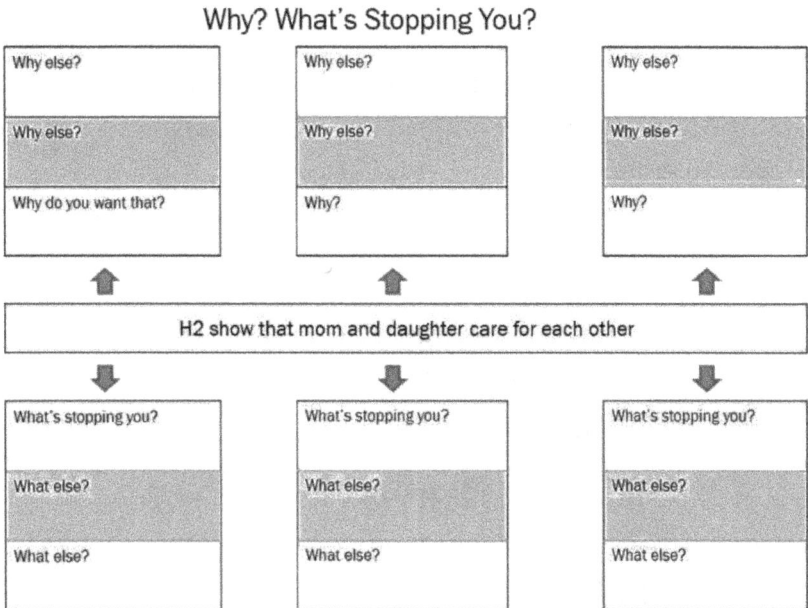

Why? What's Stopping You?

Why else?	Why else?	Why else?
Why else?	Why else?	Why else?
Why do you want that?	Why?	Why?

⬆	⬆	⬆

H2 show that mom and daughter care for each other

⬇	⬇	⬇

What's stopping you?	What's stopping you?	What's stopping you?
What else?	What else?	What else?
What else?	What else?	What else?

The trick here is to see your aspirations – your higher self – in the nine WHYs? In the nine things STOPPING YOU, you'll see your obstacles and fears. Writing them all down and forcing yourself to go deep permits you to see what often stays hidden. You have clarified the aspiration (the why's) and the problems (the what's stopping you's.)

The next thing to do is to turn those reasons (both positive and negative) into challenge statements by adding How to (H2) or How Might I (HMI) in front of your pesky problems and get your brain into thinking mode. (This is called Mighty Language. You can read more about it, on my blog here: decodingcreativity.com/mighty-language/)

Before you know it, you'll begin to have specific ideas to resolve some of those problems, and you'll be back in business again. Coming up with ideas and rolling forward smoothly.

The best thing about stopping to clarify is that you won't get stopped in your tracks when a few days, weeks, months, years later, you realize you failed to clarify. Taking the time now will help prevent your mind – and your writing – from getting muddled.

I wish you clarity, keenness, and smooth sailing.

My Ideas Are No Good

It's possible your idea is brilliant and original and you just can't see it. It's also possible your idea is clichéd and needs to be tweaked, just a bit. Either way it helps your writing flow to believe in your idea and feel inspired by it. How to get to that kind of idea? The kind that energizes you?

> ### *KM Langevin, published author...*
>
> Is a professional and published writer and is currently the Head of Content for a B2B marketing and media hub.
>
> "I'm also an aspiring novelist. When I met Julia, I already had proficient knowledge of the principles of Deliberate Creativity but never applied them to my personal writing. During this course, I learned to celebrate my idea fluency while pushing to 'the third-third' for original thinking. I now also have developmental tools in my toolbox to take my personal writing to the next level."

The Third Third Tool[xvii]

We've talked about brainstorming. When you separate divergent thinking – fun, expansive, wild, and unusual – from convergent thinking – evaluating, selecting, and perfecting – you get better ideas. Period. There are countless experiments in the peer-reviewed literature of creative studies branch of psychology, that confirm the positive contribution of this one act – consciously separating divergent and convergent thinking sessions.

As I defined, brainstorming is that one conscious choice – thinking divergently first and convergently afterward, separately. It can be you, alone at your desk coming up with ideas first, and then evaluating them. That is still brainstorming.

The Third Third hack is brainstorming on steroids. It is a method for pushing yourself to your most original ideas. Interested?

The Third Third is an ineffable concept. We cannot know how many ideas are in the set, so we cannot know how many are in a subset, or one third of the ideas. But they break out roughly like this:

First third = normal ideas

Second third = ideas start to get interesting

Third third = original thinking

When you first sit down to ideate, you come up with the normal ideas, which could be disappointing. Write them down and keep going. Your second raft of ideas start to feel good. You get a little excited. Most people stop there and move forward with one of those ideas.

The Third Third asks you to push further into wilder and more extreme ideas. Seek novelty and unusual pairings.

You'll know you're in the third third when your ideas seem... well, stupid.

Robots-in-space-having-sex-with-pirates stupid.

Keep going. Write these ideas down without judging them. Push for more and wilder ideas for your project/paragraph/plot twist/challenge.

When you're done, you're going to begin evaluating these stupid ideas. And instead of calling them stupid (even if they are) ask yourself: "How might this idea work?"

How might this idea work?

Maybe robots having sex with pirates takes on new meaning in your context, and becomes the perfect crazy dream, or video game backdrop to a somber discussion. If you thought of it, there is probably a germ of an idea that could make this highly original idea work in your context. Look at it affirmatively.

Not, "Is this a good idea?" but "How might this idea work?" It is another mighty hack that works and guides you to your most original thinking.

"IT IS EASIER TO TAME A WILD IDEA THAN IT IS TO PUSH A CLOSER-IN IDEA FURTHER OUT."

~ ALEX OSBORN

I Write 30,000 Words and Then I Quit/Stop/Get Stuck

This is the single most common complaint I hear from writers – except for the perennial "I can't find time." And I give that a full chapter in the upcoming section five: Live it - How to Quit Thinking, Feel the Feels, and Write Better

So, if this is you… you start, you're excited. You're writing and writing and then you get stuck. You get overwhelmed. You can't make the tough decisions. It's time to select and perfect. STRUCTURE hack – to the rescue!

DRIVE Hack[xviii]

You've written and written. Sometimes you've written a scene in two different documents at two different times! Once you get it all in place, you think: *huh, not bad.* And probably you like certain phrases, and some things are repetitive. How do you decide what stays and what goes? How do you *keep going* instead of giving up in the face of complexity and uncertainty?

You may think this hack is about going for a drive – and that is a perfectly cromulent way to process your thoughts and ideas. (BTW, "cromulent" is an acceptable if unexciting made-up word, courtesy of *The Simpsons)*

You have to know what you're doing. What are you creating?

When you're deciding what should be in and what should be out, use the DRIVE hack. This can be used for a single scene or the whole story. Once it's clearer what you're trying to say in your book or in your scene, the next question is simpler.

Have you said it? Is each sentence/scene necessary to further your vision?

I've adapted this hack from the DRIVE tool, used to clarify a problem in group ideation sessions, and developed by Tim Hurson. It delivers clarity on a single page, and once you've identified the criteria – what the scene/work must achieve – you know what piece parts deliver on that criterion, and which do not. You can find and cut your filler scenes and phrases.

TRY IT

Put a piece of paper horizontally, and make five columns across the top, headed by the letters: D-R-I-V-E

D = What do you want this scene (or work) to DO? What must it achieve?

R = What are the RESTRICTIONS? What must you avoid?

I = What is the reader's INVESTMENT? How willing are they to share in this scene/work? What do they need to buy in?

V= What VALUES must the characters live by in this scene/work?

E = What are the ESSENTIAL OUTCOMES? What must be relayed, understood, known by the end of the scene/work?

Simple. Clear. Definitive.

Cut liberally. Organize your scenes to press toward the vision your DRIVE hack presented.

Kathleen Cosgrove, family therapist...

is in the process of writing a memoir about her experience with adoption. "In the midst of starting a new job, I chose to participate in Decoding Creativity because I thought it would help inspire me and keep me on track to complete my first book.

After taking this class, I am confident I will reach my goals as a writer."

I Never Finish Anything

So many of us stall when it is time to put our work into the world. As writing gets tangled, or marketing gets tense, we look around and see that we are alone. There's no one out there, no one to help us. Nobody cares if we live or die.

Drama. Dread. Downer stuff.

Remember when you first had this project idea? Remember how shiny and bright it was? It was a fabulous idea, an enormous undertaking, a worthy project, that was going to change the world, or at least a small and important part of the world.

That's precisely when you should use this tool – Assisters and Resistors – while the idea is still fresh and exciting, when you really believe in its importance and impact – before you get bogged down in the crappy thoughts that are headed your way. Inevitably.

Assisters & Resistors Tool[xix]

Before you launch into your next project (or if you're still in the honeymoon phase of your current project) take a minute. Pause. Restrain yourself from diving right in. Why? Because this moment of optimism is a gift to yourself for later when you're, shall we say, less optimistic.

Take advantage of this shiny-bright-juice that is coursing through your heart and mind to clarify what obstacles you might face, and which people might help you.

It's easy. Just do it when you're still in love with your idea.

Write a list of about 100-200 people whom you know. It can start with your mom and wend its way through work acquaintances and fellow writers, and people in the industry, or your brother's cousin (if they're relevant).

Next to each name, stop and think if they will be an Assister or Resistor to your project. Give each name an A or an R – a few names might be both Assister and Resistor. (My husband is usually both.)

Resistors might include your boss, kids or your spouse, because they need you (or so they think), when you should be writing. We'll work on neutralizing resistors, in a minute.

For now, think about one small and specific thing each Assister might do to help you. There's a lot of possibilities. Let your brain range far and wide. Here's some examples:

- Introduce me to a TV development guy

- Babysit one afternoon

- Connect me to her agent

- Be a beta reader

- Talk through a plot point

- Introduce me to their meet-up group

- Transcribe from recordings

- Remind me (convince me) I'm a good writer

- Take me out for a drink

- Crack me up

- Exercise with me

- Brainstorm headlines

- Remind me I always feel this way halfway through

- Help me promote the book to his community

- Help me write a press release or produce a video news release

- Talk through how she produced her book trailer

- Like my Insta posts

- Share my FB announcement

- Download my free ebook and write a review

- Put me on their podcast

Next to the "R" people – Resistors – take a minute to think what form the resistance might take. And pre-consider how you might negate that resistance.

- Can you talk it through in advance?

- Can you make a bargain with the Resistor?

- Can you simply avoid the Resistor for a few months?

Or, for that matter, accept the resistance. Let it take up a few of your precious hours. At least then it won't come as a surprise, and you won't waste even more time in all the stewing, brewing and resentment that might follow.

RESENTMENT IS LIKE SWALLOWING POISON AND EXPECTING THE OTHER PERSON TO DIE.

~ CARRIE FISHER

Consider ideas that might take your resistors all the way to assistance. You might have a small job for them. They might like being helpful, included, acknowledged.

Assisters & Resistors tool provides a way to put your goodwill in the bank. Don't you wish you could bottle your optimism? Well, this is one way to harness the incredibly positive energy from the start of a project and store it until you need to use it. When you're down, you visit your list, and take one small step to seek help. Depending on how low you get before you seek help, you may only be up for asking someone out for a drink or a coffee. Do that one, see how you feel, then do another one.

People will embrace you. Most of us would rather help than be helped. You just have to have a small and specific suggestion as to how we might help you. Good luck!

What a difference a hack makes.

H2 Keep Writing and Feel Good

We all know that moment - that moment when there's a dissatisfaction with something large or small, or a decision that has to be made. And you fall out of the writing and begin judging the work or just feeling bad. You push back. You feel uncomfortable. Ick. Feelings. And more often than not, this is the moment when we quit writing – at least for that day. Before we even notice, we're doing something else – neatening up, checking emails, eating a brownie, watching the news. And we begin to justify the new activity, because we don't want to go back to that writing moment.

It is a good time to recenter. Before you get up from the desk. This is the CENTER tool from Dr. Eric Maisel in his book *Coaching the Artist Within*.[xx]

    <u>C –</u> ome to a complete stop.

    <u>E –</u> mpty yourself of expectation

    <u>N –</u> ame your work

    <u>T –</u> rust your resources

    <u>E –</u> mbrace the Present Moment

    <u>R –</u> eturn with Strength

When you push back from your desk and feel discouraged, try to CENTER again, using Mantras (below) that help you meet each of the actions listed above, and get you back to work, refreshed.

Each step has its mantra, said on a breath, in and out. Each mantra brings you closer to being centered and refreshed. The words below are spoken to yourself on the inhale and exhale of your breath. I use parentheses to separate the sentences into the (inhale) and (exhale) parts of your breath.

inhale (I am completely) *exhale* (stopping)

(I expect) (nothing)

(I am writing) (…) *name it*

(I trust) (my resources)

(I embrace) (this moment)

(I return) (with strength)

This can be an intervention between when you push back, and before you stand up and leave your work. The simple assertion of what I am actually doing – *inhale* (I am writing) *exhale* (my novel) – brings me out of wandering and judgmental thoughts. My resolve returns.

I return with strength.

And – *inhale* (I return) *exhale* (with strength) – never ceases to stir my soul.

Try this, breathing in on the first phrase and out on the second phrase. At the end of six deep breaths and a calming of your mind, you do, in fact, return with strength.

TAME IT RECAP

- You don't HAVE to write, but if it's something you want to do, find its value in your life. (If you write professionally and have a deadline – you have to write, right now, but it is still valuable to find its worth in your real life.)

- Hacks, tools, research – you are not alone. If you have a creative struggle, many others do too! Use a tool that thousands of people have used and whose effectiveness and impact on your thinking style is proven.

- Use the theories and tools of the science of creativity to improve your writing and writing experience

- You can achieve what you desire: *I would be great if...*

- You can see more clearly and see a clear path to the creative solution: *Why, What's Stopping You?*

- You can push yourself to your most original thinking: *The Third Third*

- And you can get out of the murky middle morass: *DRIVE tool*

- If you're someone who never finishes anything (or can't finish something you're currently working on) check your *Assistor/Resister* dashboard and get a small and specific nudge ahead.

- Change your story and your thoughts about what you're writing, so you can stay at your desk and return with strength. *Use a mantra and re-center.*

5TH STEP – LIVE IT

14 Fishoutofwater_koiquestions-CC licensed use

LIVE IT - HOW TO QUIT THINKING, FEEL THE FEELS, AND WRITE BETTER

- *How Do You Feel About Your Thoughts? What Do You Think of Your Feelings?*
- *Deliberate Creativity – It's All in How You Shift*
- *How to Stop Procrastinating and Find Time in Your Schedule*
- *The One Daily Habit (That isn't Writing) to Get Writing Flowing*
- *You Don't Have to Do it Alone*

How Do You Feel About Your Thoughts? What Do You Think of Your Feelings?

People care less about what happens in a movie or book than about how those plot twists, climaxes, and characters *made them feel.*

They never say "OMG, Seabiscuit won the race!" Or "Romeo drank the poison." They say, wow, I loved that. And they revisit those feelings. One way to get out of your head is feeling – and describing – feelings so your readers can *feel* them. How can you find and convey all the feels so people will love your work?

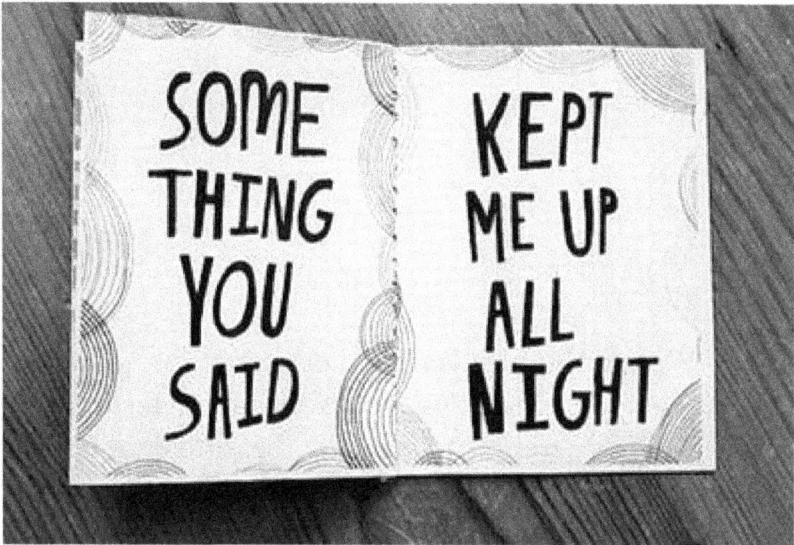

15More than feeling_by-Esempre-tempo-di-amare_CC_ PDM_1.0

<u>Thinking is in your brain. Feeling is in your body.</u>

It's amazing that thinking and feeling can share the same body. They can be at such odds with one another. Our brain has the automated hormone machine that triggers moods and feelings - forever repressing some feelings and generating others. Our ego, on autopilot, is trying to get us to believe the craven, paranoid thoughts that it's drumming up. The default setting is dis-ease.

It's part of our factory setting – our brains are looking for danger, and running comparisons, and believing other people are out to get us.[xxi] Without a strong and conscious effort, we are subject to the whims of a crazed ego. Always. But especially when we take a risk… like writing.

> *"[IT IS] OUR INHERITED DYSFUNCTION...THE MIND GENERATES SUFFERING, UN-SATISFACTORINESS, OR JUST PLAIN MISERY."*
>
> *~ ECKHART TOLLE, A NEW EARTH*

We tend to believe our thoughts at face value and allow them to subject us to unwarranted feelings. We sometimes have trouble identifying the difference between thoughts and feelings. Or understanding the origins of feelings.

There is a habit you can develop – disentangling thoughts and feelings and knowing which is true to your present situation. It takes time, support, and willingness to be present with unpleasant thoughts and feelings. If you're like me, sometimes it takes brownies (no judgment).

But this supreme mindfulness is a godsend. This is where you earn the space you need to rise above your petty thoughts and write something real. And this awareness is how you can imbue your characters with the exact same conflicts and inappropriate emotional responses – that are so human and relatable. Characters that make us *feel*.

Writing feelings...

The beautiful thing about writing is that you get to assign feelings and tell us precisely why your characters feel that way, i.e. what they're thinking – flawed or not.

In the spirit of "show, don't tell," you need to show us how they feel.

Instead of "she was mad," we like to get there with her.

"She turned on her heel. She resisted the feelings rising in her chest. She couldn't believe this was coming from her daughter. For a quick moment, she could swear she saw red."

One of the best ways to get these descriptions of feelings right is to catalog your feelings, in writing. Next time you're mad (or sad or glad or afraid) stop and write about where you feel that feeling, physically.

What does happiness feel like? And where do you actually feel it? One description...

*"HERE'S WHAT HAPPENED. I WAS IN
NEW YORK, I RAN INTO JOSH, HE MADE
ME FEEL WARM INSIDE, LIKE GLITTER
WAS EXPLODING INSIDE ME..."*

~ *CRAZY EX-GIRLFRIEND, BY RACHEL BLOOM,
ALINE BROSH MCKENNA*

Where do you feel happiness? Your heart is "lighter" in your chest? Return of energy, like you want to move, dance? Do you clap your hands in delight? Want to kiss, hug, high-five, or connect with the nearest person? Do you feel a tingle up your spine? Do you get tickled, goosebumped, shivery? Or does a smile spread across your face? Do you gasp in open-mouthed astonishment? Or is it more like, eyes closed, deep breath, grounding in a new reality?

There are a lot of ways for happiness to express itself over a fictional body – based on the events and the character. How does that feeling feel to your character? How does it show up to other characters in the scene? To your readers/audience?

Feel Good and Write Better

I've had this argument with beginners, bestsellers, reputable editors from big publishers and agents who have worked with numerous authors. People hold the belief:

If you're doing it right – writing has to be hard. It has to feel bad.
WRONG!!

I wholly disagree. Yes, most writers report that writing is H-A-A-A-R-D.

"THERE IS NOTHING TO WRITING. ALL
YOU DO IS SIT DOWN AT A TYPEWRITER
AND BLEED."

~ ERNEST HEMINGWAY

And some writers look down on those for whom it seems easy. Truman Capote was famous for saying,

---

"THAT'S NOT WRITING, THAT'S JUST
TYPING."

~ TRUMAN CAPOTE

But there are three kinds of hard (at least) …

1. Vulnerability and sharing deeply can feel hard, and truthfully, can't be helped. Art digs deep. It is hard to share your soul, question things you hold dear, and upset the world order. In this regard, good writing will always be "hard." It is demanding of its writer. Instead of thinking of this as hard, you might consider it BRAVE. It is an artist's job to be brave. We

are called to writing. We have a bravery about seeing the world differently and expressing ourselves honestly, at least on a particular topic

2. Another kind of "hard" is fear-based. Every writer faces doubts and worries or questions whether they are good enough. Whether any of this drivel you're writing matters. Fear can make your inner voice mean and facing it down is hard.

This difficulty can be nixed – and your writing sessions can be fixed. How to gain the upper hand? Presence. Being in your body. Questioning your fearful thoughts. Disengaging your ego.

Your ego wants to KNOW you're talented. It wants to be certain that the risk isn't dangerous. Put a pin in it. Talent is for others to decide. Your role is to write what you're brave enough to write the best you can. Your job is to gain support and allies in your quest to write your best, not based on whether or you're good enough or not, but because you're mortally engaged. You help and are helped. You're in a guild of writers who know your quest themselves.

This takes perspective on yourself. Presence in the moment. A willingness to question or even laugh in the face of your seemingly real fears.

This is a job for a supportive community. This is a habit you create and a muscle you strengthen over time. And there's help for that, among conscious, like-minded writers.

3. The third kind of "hard" we face is craft – our own skillset and shortcomings. There's a lot to learn about how to write well. It is a lifelong process. When I speak at writer's conferences all around the country, writers are eagerly learning dialog and scene building from experienced writers. Learning the craft is an important and valiant undertaking. At *Write Without the Fight,* we focus only on process and mindset, so your craft will elevate. You take care of the writing; we help with the process.

There's always a skill gap:

"NOBODY TELLS THIS TO PEOPLE WHO ARE BEGINNERS, I WISH SOMEONE TOLD ME. ALL OF US WHO DO CREATIVE WORK, WE GET INTO IT BECAUSE WE HAVE GOOD TASTE. BUT THERE IS THIS GAP. FOR THE FIRST COUPLE YEARS YOU MAKE STUFF, IT'S JUST NOT THAT GOOD. IT'S TRYING TO BE GOOD, IT HAS POTENTIAL, BUT IT'S

NOT. BUT YOUR TASTE, THE THING
THAT GOT YOU INTO THE GAME, IS
STILL KILLER. AND YOUR TASTE IS WHY
YOUR WORK DISAPPOINTS YOU. A LOT
OF PEOPLE NEVER GET PAST THIS
PHASE, THEY QUIT. MOST PEOPLE I
KNOW WHO DO INTERESTING,
CREATIVE WORK WENT THROUGH
YEARS OF THIS. "

~ IRA GLASS, THIS AMERICAN LIFE (NPR)

We've been there before. We all have works in the drawer that we gave up on – we hit our personal wall. That place we call "stuck" or "blocked" or just "done in." We are afraid to begin writing because that "done-in" wall awaits us. Taunts us. Like any bully, this wall says, "go ahead and try."

This is where you need new weaponry, a gang of allies, and the confidence that builds a head of steam on the journey back toward the wall. This time it's going to be different.

Why?

- Because of some of the hacks in the last chapter.

- Because of your pals in the Write Without the Fight FB group.

- Because of your newly formed view of your abilities, and newly acquired tools to fix your foibles.

- Because of your coach, pal, and fearless leader, me!

Your best writing comes from a place of hope, love, and flow. When all the risks are "out there," but not up in your face. During flow, you have created a loving space for your thoughts to roam. Sometimes, in this state, you come upon character traits and plot twists and ideas that you would never have encountered in your normal, logical, fearful writing session.

Reach flow, write with love, and embrace every word coming from your mind to your keyboard to your screen, and your writing will be at its best. You only have control over doing your best. How others respond to your writing is out of your control – whether you worry about it or not.

Choose not to worry. Write your best. Edit your best. That's a Mighty Writer.

Is this good? Does this suck?

*"TWO QUESTIONS: IS THIS GOOD?
DOES THIS SUCK?"*

~ LYNDA BARRY

As Lynda Barry says in her graphic novel-memoir-how-to-masterpiece[xxii], *What It Is? Do You Wish You Could Write?*

This simple, seemingly mature, query – "is this good?" – can be a painful, stopping thought. It changes your relationship to what you are writing. You've left divergent thinking – generating – and switched to convergent thinking – judging. From a convergent locus of thinking, it is difficult to turn your imagination back on, and go back to happily writing.

This is RULE ONE of Deliberate Creativity – as we've said before –

Separate divergent from convergent thinking

"I'M NOT SURE WHEN THESE TWO QUESTIONS BECAME THE ONLY TWO QUESTIONS I HAD ABOUT MY WORK, OR WHEN MAKING PICTURES AND STORIES TURNED INTO SOMETHING I CALLED 'MY WORK.' I JUST KNOW I'D STOPPED ENJOYING IT AND INSTEAD BEGAN TO DREAD IT."

~LYNDA BARRY

It is time to revisit Deliberate Creativity, and revisit how its guidance enters into our everyday writing.

As we recall there are four thought phases – Clarity, Ideas, Structure, and Finish.

- Each has a different creative outcome.

- Each requires a different kind of thinking.

- Each benefits from a different mindset and mood.

- Each must give way to the next thinking phase – even when the creator prefers to stall in a favored thinking phase.

- Dread is never a mood or mindset that optimizes creativity in any phase of creative thinking.

Thoughts, Feelings, and Creativity

Stuck. Blocked. Giving up. Sometimes all this pain and loss is linked to not knowing where in the creative process you are, and where you need to be. As I've said, this creative process – Deliberate Creativity, based on the Foursight Model of Creative Thinking, and earlier creative problem solving models[xxiii] – is observed and researched. This is how your brain works when creativity is working.

Deliberate Creativity – It's All In How You Shift

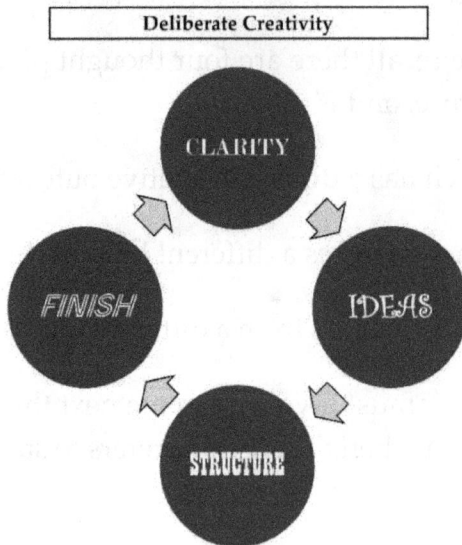

Deliberate Creativity

CLARITY

IDEAS

STRUCTURE

FINISH

You naturally proceed from one phase of thinking to the next. You naturally shift to a new thinking skill, the new feeling-state or mood, and your creativity hums along. If that's not happening, these charts can serve as a map back to the promised land.

What Do You Do in Each Phase?

Each phase of the process is defined by what is happening in that phase

- CLARITY

- IDEAS

- STRUCTURE

- FINISH

Table 8: *Deliberate Creativity – Action, per phase*

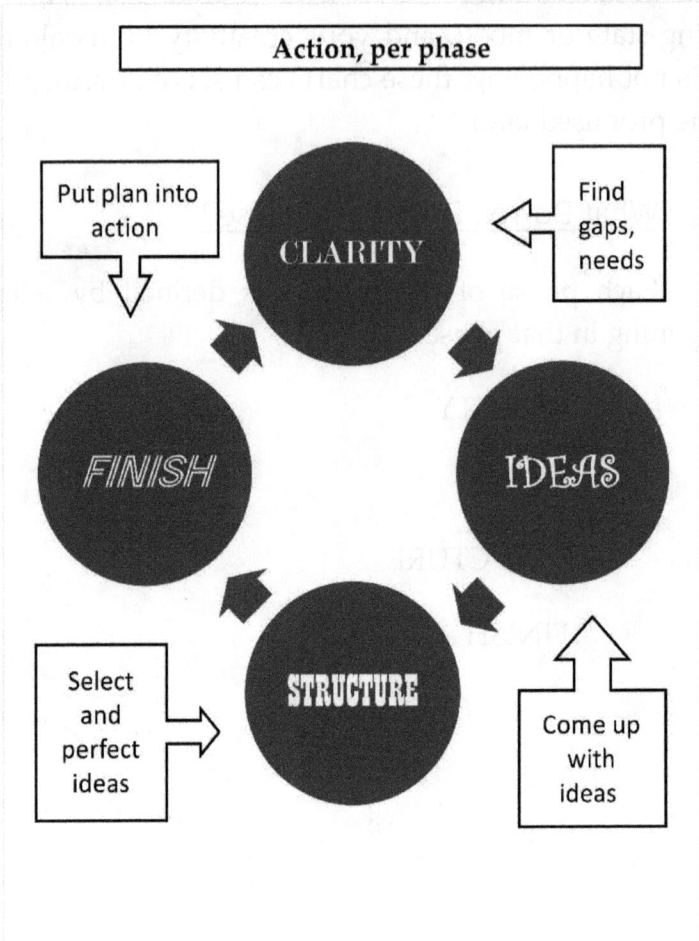

| Action, per phase |

Put plan into action

Find gaps, needs

CLARITY

FINISH

IDEAS

Select and perfect ideas

STRUCTURE

Come up with ideas

What thinking style is best in each phase?

We've identified what kind of thinking goes on in each phase. If you're stuck, you could be trying to think all wrong. ☺ What kind of thinking will this new phase of the process entail?

How can you shift?

Below you can see what thinking style serves each phase. How might you shift to continue apace? What could you do to help yourself shift from flexible (IDEAS) to decisive thinking (STRUCTURE)? Maybe a game of solitaire could help you focus in, settle down. Could playing a musical instrument shift your thinking?

Wait…Did I write this whole book to justify my solitaire habit?

Table 9: *Deliberate Creativity – Optimal Thinking Style,*
per phase

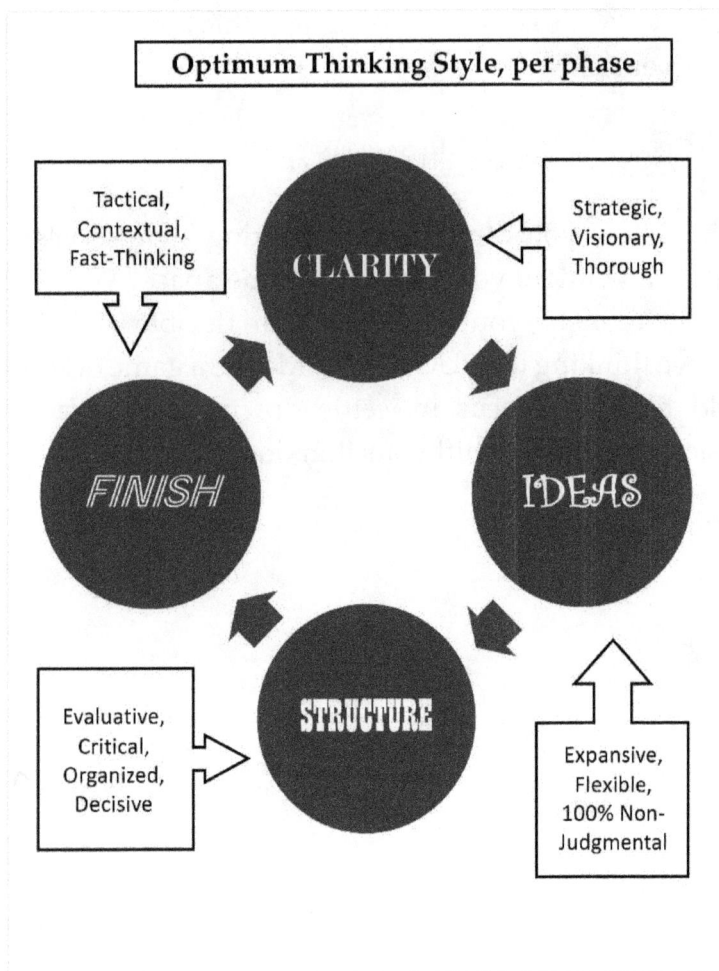

Optimum Thinking Style, per phase

Tactical, Contextual, Fast-Thinking

CLARITY

Strategic, Visionary, Thorough

FINISH

IDEAS

Evaluative, Critical, Organized, Decisive

STRUCTURE

Expansive, Flexible, 100% Non-Judgmental

Table 10: *DELIBERATE CREATIVITY – SHIFT YOUR THINKING STYLE*

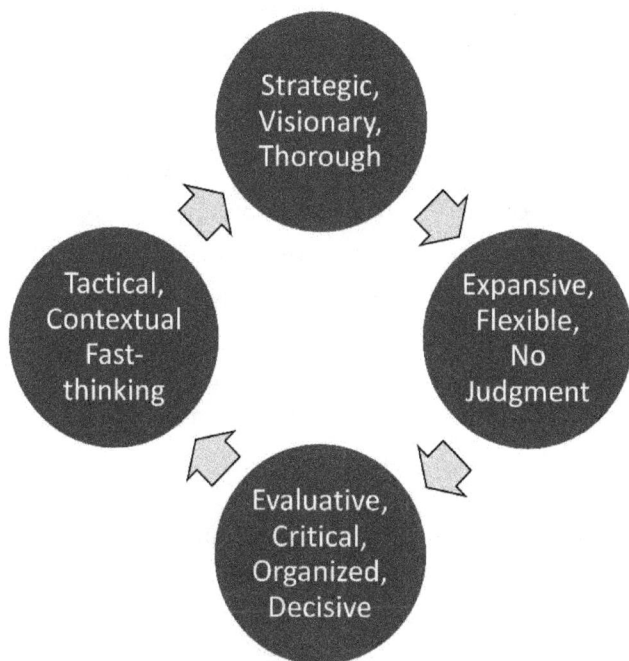

Shift Thinking Style, phase to phase

Strategic, Visionary, Thorough

Expansive, Flexible, No Judgment

Evaluative, Critical, Organized, Decisive

Tactical, Contextual Fast-thinking

What Feelings Work Best in Each Phase?

Can you write when you're in a rotten mood? If that rotten mood is caused by strong emotion, and you're writing about the cause of that emotion, you might attain a "focused, immersed" feeling, and write brilliantly. (Structure)

And yeah, sometimes it might deliver you from that mood. But not reliably. Which feelings or moods are best for productivity in each phase of creativity?

Often people can shift their thinking, but they think their mood is out of their control. Feelings *happen* to them. What might help you shift your feelings between phases? How might you go from focused-immersed feeling to opportunistic outward-looking state?

Sometimes "stuck" is just being in the wrong mood for the next phase of creating.

How could you willfully shift your mood and energy-state? Jump rope? Take a walk? A shower?

Table 11: *Deliberate Creativity – Best Feeling States, per phase*

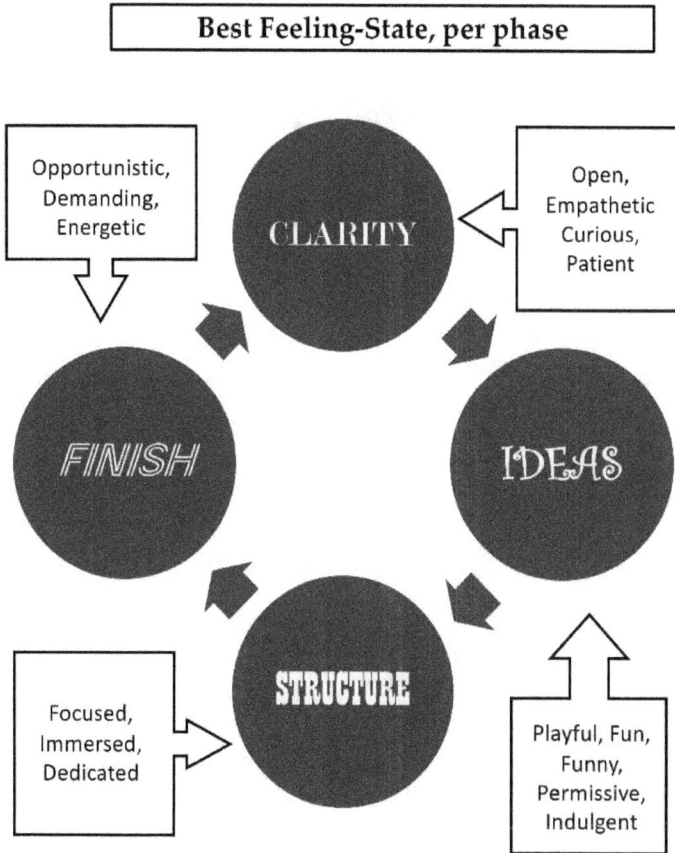

Best Feeling-State, per phase

Opportunistic, Demanding, Energetic → CLARITY

Open, Empathetic Curious, Patient → CLARITY

FINISH

IDEAS

Focused, Immersed, Dedicated → STRUCTURE

Playful, Fun, Funny, Permissive, Indulgent

Table 12: *Deliberate Creativity – Shift Your Feeling-State*

```
┌─────────────────────────────────────┐
│   Shift Feeling-State, phase to phase │
└─────────────────────────────────────┘
```

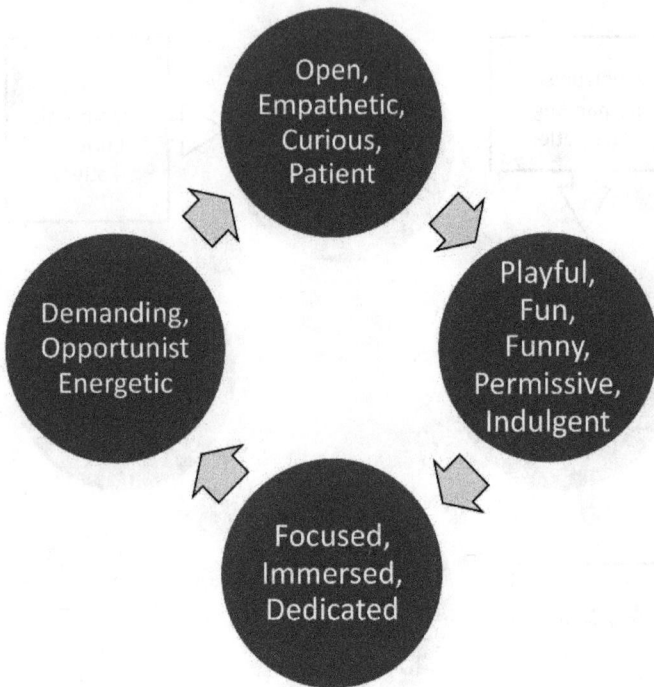

Open, Empathetic, Curious, Patient

Playful, Fun, Funny, Permissive, Indulgent

Demanding, Opportunist Energetic

Focused, Immersed, Dedicated

1. **Clarity:** How does it make you *feel* to open yourself to empathy for the characters and stakeholders in a scene or situation?

2. **Ideas:** Can you sustain a playful feeling even if you're anxious about an impending deadline?

3. **Structure:** Can you permit yourself immersion and dedication despite distractions?

4. **Finish:** Can you find fun and engagement within opportunism and feeling pushy or demanding?

How do you open yourself to curiosity? Where do you find determination? How do you feel about tolerating risk with a passion project you've been perfecting for a *very long time?*

TRY IT

Spend some time with the charts above and consider how you can shift yourself from one thinking style to another, from one feeling-state to another.

You know yourself, and if you're honest, you know you've experienced these kinds of shifts before. What has worked for you in the past? What might work in the future? Note: Sometimes shifting your thinking style will carry your mood along with it. Sometimes effecting the right feeling-state will bring your thinking style to the right place. No activity is out of bounds. TV? Taking a shower? Playing ball? These might be considered procrastination, typically, but they can also serve a distinct and useful purpose to your creative process.

Fill in the chart below, thinking about ways you might shift thinking and feeling to move yourself through the creative process productively.

Table 13: *How You Shift*

Shift	Your Activity or Method
From Clarity to Ideas	
- Thinking: *strategic* to *divergent*	
- Feeling: *patient* to *playful*	
From Ideas to Structure	
- Thinking: *expansive* to *focused*	(Ex: Solitaire could help.)
- Feeling: *funny* to *focused, immersed*	
From Structure to Finish	

- Thinking: *critical* to *fast-thinking*

- Feeling: *immersed* to *opportunistic*

From Finish to Clarity	

- Thinking: *tactical* to *strategic*

- Feeling: *demanding* to *empathetic*

Thoughts, thinking styles, and moods can all impact your ability to create in any given phase of creativity. Some moods and modes are easier for each of us. Some take effort. If you know you lose energy when you try to be playful, divergent, or extreme, then do it in short spurts. Permit yourself to use tools. Be kind to yourself.

You're a working writer, and we all push ourselves to think and feel for others, but forget to think and feel empathetically toward ourselves.

How to Stop Procrastinating and Find Time in Your Busy Schedule

16vintage-alarm-clock-thermometer_by_H-is-for-Home_CC_ BY-NC- 2.0

Stop Procrastinating

It is hard to find time for something you're dreading. But writing should not be the equivalent of a mammogram.

You can squeeze it into your day, right?

Some of you answered "no" to that question and are either feeling defiant or sulky right now. It is hard to allow for the possibility of "yes." If you answer yes, then you probably could have done that years ago. (Who wants to face down that shame?)

The easiest way to find time is to set your alarm for one or two hours earlier and write before anyone else is awake. You would be in extraordinary company. Just thinking of two great writers who have *told me* this was their stratagem:

- Khaled Hosseini, author of *Kite Runner*, worked from four am forward, and then went to work as a doctor.

- RJ Palacio, author of *Wonder*, set her alarm for three am. She worked several hours before her family woke up. They all had breakfast and then started their working and school days.

Several writers among my clients write only the hour per day that we share (up to four times a week.) One writer shifts her lunch hour to accommodate the writing commitment. Another goes into work one hour later. Some take advantage of time zone differences and are writing after work hours. You may already be thinking, "yeah, but I can't do that…" There may be *something* you could do. The question to ask yourself is:

How might I find time to write every week?

Very few of us get to write without concerns about earning a living. If you have a sponsor (like a spouse, a parent, Social Security checks, or a king) take advantage of this time in your life! Write.

YOU get to decide how you spend your day, your hours, your minutes. You're a free, adult person who likes to write. Let's get you writing.

Turkey Soup

This is a true story of pure procrastination. When I was in my twenties, living with my boyfriend, we got a free turkey from the grocery store at Thanksgiving. I roasted it and we ate and ate. We were pretty broke at the time, so having turkey in the house was a dream come true. I was determined to make turkey soup with the carcass. I wanted to try my hand at it, though I'd never done it before. My mom made broths and soups when I was growing up. I boiled the turkey and let it cool. The next thing would have been to pick the meat off the bones and add veggies and noodles. Therein lay the procrastination. I let days go by. Many days. By the time I faced down this icky challenge of removing the meat from the bones, the turkey reeked. It stunk up the whole apartment.

I felt so bad about procrastinating and wasting this turkey, that I picked that stinky meat from those stinky bones and tried to make a stinky soup out of it. Denial. I could not however get my boyfriend to even try the stinky soup. I had to throw it out. Why'd I drag myself through that? It is hard to admit we're procrastinating, and harder to admit we're stupidly self-sabotaging.

Procrastinating is a kind of block. It permits you to think you have a fun, simple problem – "I'm such a procrastinator!" – instead of a deeper, more painful problem – "I'm blocked and have been for years."

And as we've discussed, you cannot bully yourself into creating. You must lead yourself into it with some expectation of joy and magic.

To achieve that expectation, realistically, you need to shift your energy. You need to upshift. You need to feel lighter, more playful, more open to a vision and ideas.

Often this shift comes from being physical – like taking a walk, puttering around the house, or taking a shower. Sometimes it can come from another creative undertaking.

Einstein played violin when physics answers eluded and frustrated him. He called it combinatory play. I call it Procrastubation.

If you've tried some of these tactics, and are still procrastinating, try them again, without judging yourself. It is the judgment that creates delays, not the activities.

For *57 Ways to Stop Procrastinating* – each of them easy to do and grounded in science – visit https://go.decodingcreativity.com/57-ways.

Let Yourself Write.

We're all busy – SO BUSY! We live in our cars, we dine at the drive-thru, we consider time in the dental chair "ME" time. Who are you if you're not busy?

The Busy Badge

You've earned your Busy Badge.You can hold your head high in the endless To-Do List Showdown that we all engage in. Who's busiest? Whose life is the most impossible? (Though, miraculously, we pull it off.) It's not enough that we are busy, but we have to prove it to others.

Why? To impress and intimidate each other? To placate the (scared, defensive, petty) ego inside each of us.

Yet, *busy* is sort of a derogatory word. It doesn't connote the same power of words like engaged, leading, active, building, productive, or effective.

People strive to be busy, thinking it will bring them success. Busy, in their minds, equals sought-after, important, and needed.

During a pregnancy, you sometimes have something called false labor. It hurts like a sonofabitch but it's not the real thing. The difference between true and false labor is its product. You want your labor, as difficult and consuming as it is, to be fruitful.

Don't be busy for busy's sake. Be fruitful.

TRY IT

Look at your To-Do list. If you do not have a current list, create one now. Don't reserve a mental list of smaller everyday items. Write them all down. Spend some time to make sure that everything you feel you need to do is on this one list.

Now look at your full list.

Circle the tasks that you will be glad you did, one year from now

- Because they will build toward something you want

- Because they will make a difference in your life, or the lives of people you love

This is true labor.

The remainder of the tasks – the false labor – may be tasks you can choose not to do.

Put an X through the tasks you'd like to be rid of. Then consider ways to skip, skimp, or discard those jobs.

I'VE SEEN WOMEN INSIST ON CLEANING EVERYTHING IN THE HOUSE BEFORE THEY COULD SIT DOWN TO WRITE...AND YOU KNOW, IT'S A FUNNY THING ABOUT HOUSECLEANING. IT NEVER COMES TO AN END. PERFECT WAY TO STOP A WOMAN.

A WOMAN MUST BE CAREFUL NOT TO LET OVER-RESPONSIBILITY (OR OVER-RESPECTABILITY) STEAL HER NECESSARY CREATIVE RIFFS, RESTS AND RAPTURES. SHE SIMPLY NEEDS TO PUT HER FOOT DOWN AND SAY NO TO ABOUT HALF OF WHAT SHE THINKS SHE

"SHOULD" BE DOING. ART IS NOT
MEANT TO BE CREATED IN STOLEN
MOMENTS ONLY.

~ DR. CLARISSA PINKOLA ESTES

Is it Too Late?

It's never too late unless you don't start. Some authors didn't even publish until after their 40th birthdays. (That's not an excuse for you to wait until you're 40! My first book was published when I was 44.)

Here's a list of 15 authors who published after 40, and still had enormous success. (Because you can Google anything and feel better, or way worse, LOL)

AT THE AGE OF 40 -

1. George Eliot's first novel: *Adam Bede*, and Eliot went on to write six more novels, including *Middlemarch*, though she only lived to 61. (Start now.)

2. William S. Burroughs' first book, *Junky*. *Naked Lunch* bowed six years later.

AT THE AGE OF 41 -

3. Mark Twain published his first novel, *The Adventures of Tom Sawyer*

At 43?

4. Bram Stoker published his first novel, *The Snake's Pass*, when he was 43. He published *Dracula* when he was 50.

5. Marcel Proust didn't publish the first volume of *À la Recherche du Temps Perdu* until he was 43.

Is 44 too late? 45?

6. Henry Miller's first book, *Tropic of Cancer* was too risqué for the US, so it was published in France, first, when Miller was 44.

7. Alex Haley's *The Autobiography of Malcolm X* was published when he was 44. *Roots*, his second book, came out when he was 55.

8. J. R. R. Tolkien's first novel, *The Hobbit*, was published when he was 45 years old. He wrote the *Lord of the Rings* trilogy over the next ten years. It was published when he was 63.

9. Tony Hillerman published *The Blessing Way* when he was 45.

Can you still get started in your 50's? Or is that too late?

10. Raymond Chandler, the creator of the Philip Marlowe character, pub'd his first novel, *The Big Sleep*, when he was 51.

11. *Watership Down* was an instant classic, by Richard Adams, pub'd when he was 52.

12. Annie Proulx gave us *Postcards* when she was 57. *The Shipping News* was published a year later.

13. Daniel Defoe gave us his debut novel, *Robinson Crusoe*, at age 59.

60 IS THE NEW 40. GET GOING!

14. When Laura Ingalls Wilder was 65 years old, her first book *Little House in the Big Woods*, was published. Her *Little House* series ran eight novels, published throughout her 70's. A partial book, *The First Four Years*, was found after her death and published in 1971.

15. *Angela's Ashes* came out when author Frank McCourt was 66. The film was produced and in theaters three years later.[xxiv]

When you have a story to tell, it is never too late.

Find Time

Time, money, and closet space – three things we can never have enough of, or so goes the common wisdom. How do we manage to make, justify, and *take the time* for writing?

"Not enough" is the clarion call of the lizard brain – and his Top 10 Tunes of fear and sparcity. (See chart below: *Table 14: Top Ten Tunes of the Lizard Brainthe Lizard Brain*) Do you have enough money? How much is enough? Do you have enough closet space? How much are you trying to keep closeted? Do you have enough time to write? Many of us don't let ourselves write. It doesn't seem worth the time.

How much time do you need? Some would say the more important consideration is what *kind* of time you need?

- Sometimes, you need focus. Expectation. Engagement. Flow.

- Other times, you need play, fun, self-indulgence

How much of that can you achieve in half-hours here and there? Or an hour each morning? Plenty. What's most important about using the time you have is shifting gears (mood and mindset) to the right mode for the phase of creativity.

Consciously shift. Consciously choose to submerge. Ask your brain to "show me," as Bill Kenower suggests, and take a minute to remember what flow feels like. Feeling it is half of what it takes to get there.

Once Upon a Time

Once upon a time, I worked around the clock in a crazy, demanding job that made me feel important. I was in charge of the Burger King account at a young age and *RAN* through my life. I was pretty sure I had zero time. And that ALL my time was spoken for. And I was basically right. I was at the office till two a.m. some days and flying to Chicago or Miami most weeks. After another "crisis" and a heated round of the blame game, I gave my notice. We agreed that I would stay to finish the project, but then I left, with a negotiated severance bonus.

Suddenly, I had walked through a time portal. All my time was mine. Did I write a book? No. I did not.

I'm not saying "no time" was just an excuse, it was real. I was way too busy to write. I was too busy to pee, half the time. But it was also a shallow excuse. The reason I wasn't writing wasn't actually time. There was something deeper. My whole life wasn't my own. And, wanting to find time to write might have been a single note, but a strong pull back toward balance and boundaries for me.

Until you give yourself time on a regular basis you won't confront your deeper reasons for stopping yourself.

Time is relative. Time is yours. You can only know your potential by investing time in writing, in embracing yourself, in facing your fears and letting yourself expand.

Dianne Irving, children's book publisher

Has the dearest memories of reading bedtime stories to her son when he was little. It is her passion to create the kind of book parents and children can bond over, pore over and read again and again. She is an artist, children's book writer and publisher with Little Tulip Books.

What the club does for her? "We're constantly looking at different layers of obstacles and ways to move through them. It is utterly liberating to me."

The One Daily Habit (That Isn't Writing) to Get Your Best Work Flowing

READ AND WRITE FOUR TO SIX HOURS A DAY. IF YOU CANNOT FIND THE TIME FOR THAT, YOU CAN'T EXPECT TO BECOME A GOOD WRITER.

~ STEPHEN KING

So much pressure to write every day. In fact, if you don't write every day, forget about it. Right? Do you have to write every day? Are there other models that work? Of course there are. But many will insist it's the only way forward.

Think about Thinking

Q: What is the one thing you can do, daily, to make your brain and creativity most available to you?

A: Hold awareness of what you're thinking.

Like watching a movie with subtitles, be at least somewhat aware of your thoughts and how they're affecting your creativity, mood, productivity, and inspiration.

See what problems and solutions your brain offers.

When you "get" an idea out of the blue, where did it come from? Had you unconsciously ordered a solution to that problem? Was your brain working on an idea, diligently, in the background while you cooked, gardened, rode your bike?

Self with a Capital 'S'

Most of us, writers in particular, think we *are* our thoughts. Our brain is what makes us *us*. And to a degree, that's true. Our brain is a lot of what makes you unique, but your thoughts are often mundane, cookie-cutter fears. And your self-bullying is straight out of an ancient playbook.

I say "ancient" because these thoughts and fears stem from our earliest brain evolution – sometimes called the Lizard brain.

Dr. Martha Beck (*Finding Your Own North Star*) has narrowed it down to the Top 10 Tunes of Lizards everywhere.[xxv]

Table 14: *Top Ten Tunes of the Lizard Brain*

- I'll never find love.

- Oh no! I don't have enough...

- People want to take my...

- I can't be perfectly happy, until…

- People are looking at me.

- Everybody pressures me to …

- You just can't trust…

- People will hurt me unless I…

- If only I had… If only I were…

- I must hang onto…

Do you recognize your fears anywhere in there? Artists have another resounding (and fairly universal) fear.

You think you're good enough? Who do you think you are?

The thought turnarounds we discussed in *Honor How You Create and Think* can help you dismantle these gripping (if unoriginal) thoughts.

Be Original

It is refreshing and original for someone to be at peace within themselves. This peace becomes purpose, which becomes power. And it shows in everything you write, everywhere you go.

The one habit that can help you write at your best is to be aware of your thoughts. "You" are above your thoughts. You are Self with a capital "S." This Self is at peace. This is your core, and it lives without fear, pain, or indecision. It just is.

Your Self is there, in the driver's seat, driving you to your stated and logical goals. Your thoughts – fearing risk, vulnerability, change, and humiliation – will take over the driving if it can, or sabotage the bus, if it can't. On the other side, your "saint" is trying to keep you perfect, performing, and conforming, and will definitely scold, shame, or bully you to keep you on the straight and narrow. Keep you from taking risks, even artistic risks.

See your thoughts as separate from your Self. You are the master, who can see the little, fearful, wild-child throwing a tantrum. You can also see the dictator-bitch calling you on the carpet. They both want to serve you and are doing the best they can, but their limitations hold them back, so they don't usually give you the best advice.

Thank them. Consider if there is a germ of truth to what they demand. "How might this be helpful?" Then, hold your position in the driver's seat. Move progressively toward your desired dream.

Use Your Brain Wisely

17Flickr, licensed-cc-use

The one life-altering habit is to use your brain instead of abusing it.

- Capture new ideas on your phone or a small pad

- Interrupt fearful or painful or bullying thoughts and question their veracity

- Flood your brain periodically with sunshine and light thoughts

- Catch yourself in judgment and question your conclusions.

"THE MIND IS AN EXCELLENT SERVANT, BUT A TERRIBLE MASTER."

~ LAO-TSU

You Don't Have to Do It Alone

You can do it with us. Day after day, week after week, year over year. You can put regular writing into your life. You can publish, produce, submit, perform the things you're writing.

Isolation

Isolation lowers our ability to cope well. And writing is all about coping. We have to cope with anxieties, other demands on our time, and meeting our and others' expectations. Then we have to cope with all the situations our characters get into and have to get out of. We are working on a complex puzzle, with many moving parts.

Clarity, character, plot, humor, and tension... they can immerse you, and isolate you from the world you're living in.

Writers feel isolated all the time. We are weirdos. We are often *delightful* weirdos, but weirdos, nonetheless. It might feel good to be non-conforming, but also isolating when you feel the need to fit in or want to be better understood.

> "HUMANS ARE HARDWIRED TO INTERACT WITH OTHERS, ESPECIALLY DURING TIMES OF STRESS. WHEN WE GO THROUGH A TRYING ORDEAL ALONE, A LACK OF EMOTIONAL SUPPORT AND FRIENDSHIP CAN INCREASE OUR ANXIETY AND HINDER OUR COPING ABILITY."
>
> ~ PSYCHOLOGY TODAY xxvi

Writers are the best weirdos.

In case you doubt the perils of isolation – you're an introvert, as many writers are, and embrace alone time – I bring up two fictional examples:

1. Consider Tom Hanks in *Cast Away*.[xxvii] He named a volleyball "Wilson" and treated it like his best friend. Do you have a "Wilson"?

Isolation can cause us to form attachment to routines, surroundings, things. We can feel aversion to change. (BTW, if you *need* it, the real volleyball was just retrieved from the ocean, 19 years after the shooting of the movie.)

2. And do not forget "Here's Johnny" in *The Shining*.[xxviii] Jack Torrance (played by Jack Nicholson) was objectively terrifying.

ALL WORK AND NO PLAY MAKES JACK A DULL BOY.
ALL WORK AND NO PLAY MAKES JACK A DULL BOY.
ALL WORK AND NO PLAY MAKES JACK A DULL BOY.
ALL WORK AND NO PLAY MAKES JACK A DULL BOY.
ALL WORK AND NO PLAY MAKES JACK A DULL BOY.
ALL WORK AND NO PLAY MAKES JACK A DULL BOY.

Writers need time alone – lots of it. But we also need to know that there are people around us. Engaged, available, supportive people.

Do you agree or disagree? Tell us why in the Write Without the Fight free FB group.

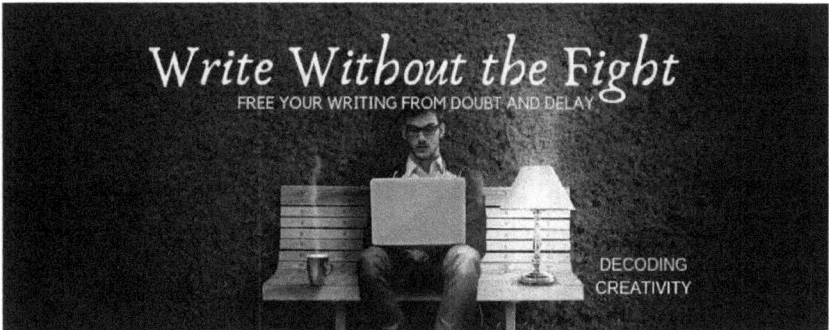

Write Without the Fight
FREE YOUR WRITING FROM DOUBT AND DELAY

DECODING
CREATIVITY

Mighty Writers Club

Susan Koziak, event producer, screenwriter

had a unique and powerful story to tell. It had been knocking on her brain for years and years. She wanted it written.

"Julia helped me in so many areas, to redirect and use the time I have, but more productively. Mostly she helped me dismantle the stories I have been telling myself that would normally keep me from writing and learn to be kinder to myself and not beat myself up when I don't always do what I say I'm going to do."

A bit more about the Mighty Writers Club – because that is the heart of my business, my people, where I invest my time, my concern, my training and coaching, week after week. This club is my passion. These writers are my people. And what we are each writing is important!

Good coaching costs $200 an hour. Book coaching mentorships are skyrocketing to $25,000 a year. These clubs promise "bestseller status" because they've learned how to manipulate the Amazon systems to propel your book, however briefly, into a #1 position.

How do I know? I joined a course like that, and published my Masters thesis as a book, *Sex, Lies and Creativity – Gender Differences in Creative Thinking,* and I got to #1 ranking in several categories. And it was fun. I took a million screenshots. I was ahead of Daniel Pink, for goodness' sake.

- These groups aren't about good writing. They're about publishing.

- Mind you, there's nothing wrong with publishing!

- These groups are intended to help non-writers create a business book, a big business card, and to achieve "bestseller" status.

In the Mighty Writers Club, we're here in support of writers, who may or may not be writing when they start the club, but for whom writing is not just something they do, it's something they identify with. In our club, we also work toward and share knowledge about how to publish, build an audience, find an agent, blog, submit article and short stories and win awards, too.

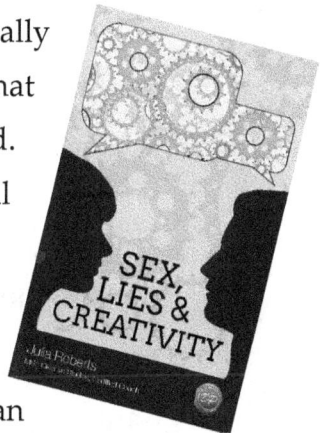

And, yes, it feels nice to officially be a bestseller. But these days that concept is severely cheapened. Achieving this status did not fulfill my lifelong dream. I still want to be a *New York Times* bestseller and have a novel made into a movie. This is NOT the same as having an Amazon bestseller for a day or two and have my book made into a youtube trailer. (You can see the book trailer, for *Sex, Lies & Creativity* @ youtube.com/watch?v=7alSVRti06Q)

The Mighty Writers Club is about writing. It is about overcoming the things holding you back. It is about improving your relationship with your creativity. It is about bettering yourself so you can write the best you have in you.

It is about aiming for that lifelong dream with all you've got. We discuss:

- Publishing, epubbing, hybrid pubbing

- Finding an agent

- Book cover and interior design

- Story structure

- Pre-order sales

- Medium

- Creative Process

- Creativity/unblocking tools & tricks

- And every other question that arises within our group

This is your club. Where you fit in, unapologetically. Here's where you know the secret handshake, get the inside jokes, and know your way around.

The Mighty Writers Club is a group of people who write, seriously. They are learning about the creative process and their creative thinking profile and applying it as they work. They are getting things written that they want done. They're making their voices heard in the world.

This Mighty Writers Club is where you can figure out precisely where your creative process takes a turn for the worse. But more importantly, it helps you learn where you can get support and and expert guidance. Emotional and practical help. You won't need to decipher a chart – you'll have science on your side.

This is also how you can validate what you do well so you can lean into it. Modesty is overrated. Self-awareness and self-knowledge are empowering. Liberating. And knowing yourself better can help you write better characters. For more on joining us, go here. Yay, Mighty Writers!

"IF THERE IS A BOOK THAT YOU WANT TO READ, BUT IT HASN'T BEEN WRITTEN YET, YOU MUST BE THE ONE TO WRITE IT."

~ TONI MORRISON

You Don't Have to Do It Alone

There's no shortage of examples to support the notion that writing is hard.

What if we find a way to incorporate fun, self-knowledge, fascination and triumph? Could you write your best? Some (many) writers would scoff at this notion. They firmly believe writing is hard. Should be hard.

Yes, you'll dig deep. Yes, you will need to be brave and work hard. Yes, you will need to put in your days writing. It may not be for everyone, but does it have to be hard?

It may be hard to maintain optimism, hope, and perspective when you're facing your forever long to-do.

You don't have to do it alone.

Whatever you write has the capacity to be bigger than you, and bigger than you can even imagine. Alone, you may not see or believe its destiny.

You can do it with us.

*"THE PURPOSE OF ART IS NOT THE
RELEASE OF A MOMENTARY EJECTION
OF ADRENALINE BUT IS, RATHER, THE
GRADUAL, LIFELONG CONSTRUCTION
OF A STATE OF WONDER AND
SERENITY."*

~ GLENN GOULD

LIVE IT RECAP

- The simplest thing to remember about thoughts and feelings is that thoughts are in our brains, and feelings are in our bodies. This is true of ourselves and our characters. When you *feel* something, stop thinking. Focus on where the feeling is in your body, and how you feel it. Describe it to yourself, with empathy.

- Is procrastination ok? Is it a laziness? Fear? If you feel ashamed of procrastinating, the likely outcome is that the shame will prolong the procrastination timeframe.

- There are many ways to actually exploit procrastination to reboot your creativity. (Don't judge it!)

- To master Deliberate Creativity – you must *deliberately* be aware of how you're thinking, of your mood, and how you might shift from one thinking mode to another, or one mood to another. And how to use the Deliberate Creativity model to know which thinking mode and mood is appropriate for optimum creativity.

- Deliberate Creativity is based on the research and models of great scientists and especially the model Foursight Creative Thinking Model developed by Dr. Gerard Puccio, chair of the International Center for Creative Studies at Buffalo State College. I've tweaked its name and representation to make it more accessible to writers and other individual creators.

- Let yourself write. It's okay. It's okay to write intermittently, in the morning, in the nights, on weekends, once in a while. Writing is its own reward.

The one daily habit that is essential to creativity is awareness of your thinking – like reading subtitles in a movie. You're thinking, hearing and feeling your thought, but you're also "reading" it – aware that it is not you. You are above your thoughts. And when you can see your thoughts, you can choose truer thoughts.

Don't be isolated. Find company, empathy, and support, whether or not it is with us.

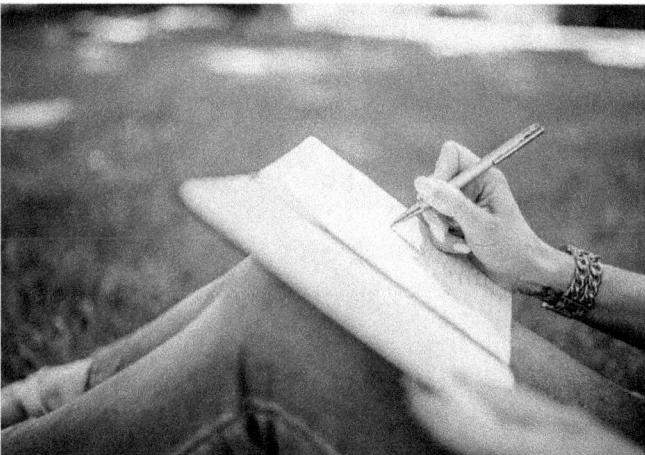

Review

- *How is This going to Help Me Write Better?*
- *What Tools and Concepts Did We Cover?*
- *Where Can I Learn Even More?*

Congratulations. We have covered a lot of territory, and you're on your way to understanding some creativity theory and how to maximize your brain to optimize your writing ability.

How is This Going to Help Me Write Better?

I'm not sure what your personal challenge within the creative process might be, because we each have our own stumbling blocks. Does any of this seem like you?

- You write and quit.

- You think you should write but you don't get started.

- You research forever but never feel ready to start.

- You rush your work and are selling it before it's finished.

- You get overwhelmed and lose your opportunity.

- You write and edit and write – and end up with overworked copy, and zero confidence.

The creative thought process is universal. Writers and creative people are anything but universal.

We each flow and bump. Go and stall. We'd like our rough edges to become "gears" instead, so they can click into the creative process and fit instead of fight that cyclical motion.

We are each great at something about writing – enough to love doing it. We can use Deliberate Creativity to help us protect the part we love by giving us a way through the parts we struggle with. Bring your great research, your brilliant idea, your perfect editing, your great opportunity from notion to known. Share what you have and benefit the world.

Deliberate Creativity can take your inner baby – your most creative thinking skill – and give it wings, or a parachute and a landing strip – depending on what it needs.

That's how Deliberate Creativity can help you write better. It protects what you do well, and powers you (and your creation) through to finished.

What Tools and Concepts Did We Cover?

- You learned the power of "might" and why we're called Mighty Writers.

- You, hopefully, banished the word "lazy" from your mind and redefined "busy."

- For some of you, this is the first time you ever heard of a Masters in Creativity! It is a great degree, and I'm happy to talk to you about it. Ask me in the WWTF FB Group.

- You learned that the CIA was behind the early research that bolsters our understanding of how to measure and enhance our creative abilities.

- You saw Deliberate Creativity and what the cycle of your creative musings looks like when you're being brilliant.

- You learned to see (and turn around) your fearful/painful/stopping thoughts.

- You disentangled thinking and feeling – and learned which of each come in handy in what phases of creative thinking.

- We saw the map of creative thinking, and where and when to shift both thinking and feeling states for optimum creating.

- We tackled two of the most common complaints I hear in my FB group and from my clients:

o How to quit procrastinating

o How to find the time to write

- We learned four excellent hacks to help you all the way through the creative cycle.

- We tackled how to keep writing with a powerful mantra.

- We shared how to get help when you need it most.

We share creative space in the Mighty Writers Club – we work regularly together, to write up to four times a week, and talk twice a month to shake off obstacles, learn new things, and build an audience as we write. And inside the "Clubhouse," there's a plethora of information on the creative process, publishing and promoting your work.

The world will be bettered when you weirdos get your act together and write!

You're brilliant. Go be you. We're waiting for you.

WHERE CAN I LEARN EVEN MORE?

Get on my mailing list! And, I'll reward you with a free MIGHTY LITTLE BOOK – *10 Ways to Find Time to Write and Other Magic Tricks* (You can unsubscribe any time, but I like to bring tools and tips to the people who stick around.) Use: https://go.decodingcreativity.com/10-ways-time.

I've mentioned a bunch of ways to work with me in the course of this book. I want more writers to be empowered to write at their best. So, sue me. All year long, there are ways to get help from me free and at low cost –

- The Write Without the Fight FB Group
  @https://fb.com/groups/wwtfgroup

- 5-Day Write Without the Fight Challenge (2x a year)
  @https://go.decodingcreativity.com/5-day

- 57 Ways to Stop Procrastinating
  @ https://go.decodingcreativity.com/57-ways

- Workshops are offered regularly in the FB group – look for ones that focus on your struggle! (But they're all worthwhile!)

- The Mighty Writers Club is a bit of an investment – but still designed to be affordable for as long as it takes you to write your book or script. And of course, once you invest in yourself and your writing – the dividends are invaluable! Learn more @ https://go.decodingcreativity.com/mighty

Julia is invited as a featured "salon speaker"
on the TEDx stage in Summer 2022 – look for & watch:
"It's Not Just Mojo, The Surprising Science of Creativity"

WRITERS R
THE BEST
WEIRDOS♥

DECODING CREATIVITY

ACKNOWLEDGEMENTS

My gratitude goes to so many for the achievement of this "indie" published book! The energy and selfless contributions have been many! Thanks to early readers and reviewers – I couldn't do it without you.

Thanks to Paper Raven Books and others who held my hand on this long technical path to published.

In the creativity arena, I stand on many shoulders, my teachers at Buffalo State – especially Susan Keller, John Cabra, Cyndi Burnett, Blair Miller, Russ Schoen, and of course, Dr. Gerard Puccio. And Tim Hurson, co-founder of Mindcamp. I'd like to thank Josh Mahaney, Jody Reed Fisher and the Creative Education Foundation for helping me source and credit creativity tools.

I'm shaped and helped by my coaching mentors, Dr. Martha Beck and Dr. Eric Maisel.

Joel Madison, your humor has always charmed me. Thank you for the foreword.

I would be remiss if I didn't mention Amy Brockway. Thank you for saving me with last minute, urgent graphic changes.

Cecily Roberts stepped in to design the book cover – something that should always be done by a professional -

and my husband Adam Philips read, edited, proofread and pitched in on anything that overwhelmed me throughout the process. My daughter Lucy Philips-Roberts had an opinion about everything. Sophie and Freddy Philips-Roberts supported in a more "hands-off" way. Appreciated. I am lucky to have such caring and capable people in my life.

LIST OF PHOTOGRAPHS & CREDITS

Endnotes

[i] G.J. Puccio, M. Mance, M.C. Murdock, B. Miller, J. Vehar, R. Firestien, S. Thurber, & D. Nielsen; *Models of Creative Thinking: CPS Model*; Buffalo, NY: International Center for Studies in Creativity (2011). "Creative Problem Solving" generates variations on the method can be traced back to the work of Alex Osborn in the 1940s, developed with Sid Parnes in the 1950s, and nurtured at SUNY Buffalo State and the Creative Education Foundation.

[ii] Gerard J. Puccio, Cyndi Burnett, Selcuk Acar, Jo A. Yudess, Molly Holinger John F. Cabra, *The Journal of Creative Behavior,* Vol. 54, Iss. 2, pp. 453–471 Scituate, MA: Creative Education Foundation (2018); Sidney Parnes and Ruth Noller, *Creative Studies Project* conducted ground-breaking research demonstrating that students trained in divergent thinking techniques were able to produce twice as many quality ideas as those who did not have creativity training. (1970's)

[iii] Dave Meier, *The Accelerated Learning Handbook, A Creative Guide to Designing and Delivering Faster, More Effective Training Programs,* New York: McGraw Hill, (2000).

[iv] P. Maclean *Triune Brain,* (1990, and 1952) as inspired by Papez (1937)

[v] Elizabeth Gilbert, *Big Magic,* New York: Penguin Publishing Group; (2016)

[vi] Mihayli Csikszentmihalyi, *Flow, The Psychology of Optimal Experience,* London, UK: Ebury Press, (2002)

[vii] William Kenower, *Fearless Writing, How to Create Boldly and Write with Confidence,* Cincinnati, OH: Writers Digest Books (2017)

[viii] Alec Osborne, *Applied Imagination: Principles and Procedures of Creative Problem Solving*, New York: Charles Scribner's Sons, (1953)

[ix] Alec Osborne, *Applied Imagination*, (1953); Also noted, Hindu teachers had been using brainstorming for over 400 years and Walt Disney encouraged it among his artists in the 1920s (later called "dreaming as a team"). Osborn formalized the tool in the 40s.

[x] G.J. Puccio et al; *Models of Creative Thinking: CPS Model* (2011)

[xi] FourSight™ is a valid, research-based assessment tool developed over the last 20 years by Gerard Puccio, Ph.D., director of the International Center for Studies in Creativity at the State University of New York College at Buffalo. Dr. Puccio is dedicated to teaching the "science" of creativity and innovation to graduate students and business professionals to help them gain awareness, skills and mastery of the creative process.

FourSight is the assessment tool he developed to telegraph the Center's fundamental discoveries and principles around creativity and innovation to a broader audience.

[xii] Byron Katie, *Loving What Is, Four Questions that Can Change Your Life,* New York: Three Rivers Press (2003)

[xiii] Anne Lamott, *Bird by Bird, Some Instruction on Writing and Life,* New York: Anchor, 1994

[xiv] William Kenower, *How to Create Boldly and Write with Confidence,* Cincinnati, OH: Writers Digest Books (2017)

xv A. Isaakson, D. Treffinger, Creative Problem Solving: The Basic Course. Buffalo, NY: Bearly Limited (1985); J. Cabra, R. Schoen (2011)

xvi Why? What's Stopping You Tool: S.I. Hayakawa in 1978, based on the work of A. Korzybski in 1933. Sidney Parnes, Optimize the Magic of Your Mind. Buffalo, NY: Bearly Limited (1997). S. Isaksen, B. Dorval, & D. Treffinger, Creative Approaches to Problem Solving: A Framework for Change (2nd. Ed.). Williamsville, NY: Creative Problem Solving Group-Buffalo (2000)

xvii Min Basadur, Ron Thompson, Usefulness of the Ideation Principle and Extended Effort in Real World Professional and Managerial Creative Problem Solving; Hamilton, ON, Canada: McMaster University; Calgary, ALB, Canada: University of Calgary, (1983) xviii Tim Hurson, Think Better: The Innovators Guide to Productive Thinking. New York, NY: McGraw-Hill (2008).

xix J. Cabra, R. Schoen, Buffalo State College (2011)

xx Eric Maisel, Ph.D., Coaching the Artist Within, Novato, CA: New World Library (2005)

xxi Eckhart Tolle, A New Earth – Awakening to Your Life's Purpose, New York: Penguin (1998)

xxii Lynda Barry, What It Is, Do You Wish You Could Write? Montreal, QUE, Canada: Drawn and Quarterly; Illustrated edition (2008)

xxiii G.J. Puccio et al., Models of Creative Thinking: CPS Model (2011).

xxiv Erica Verillo, Blog: *Published to Death* https://publishedtodeath.blogspot.com/2017/11/15-famous-authors-who-were-published.html (11/12/2017)

xxv Martha Beck, Ph.D., *Finding Your Own North Star, Claiming the Life You Were Meant to Live*, New York: Three Rivers Press (2001)

xxvi S. Sreenivasan, Ph.D., and L. Weinberger, Ph.D., *Psychology Today*, online edition; https://www.psychologytoday.com/us/blog/emotional-nourishment/202112/belonging-why-humans-want-fit-in (12/6/2021)

xxvii Feature film, *Cast Away,* 20th Century Fox (2000)

xxviii Feature film, *The Shining*, Warner Bros (1980) based on the novel *The Shining*, by Stephen King, New York: Doubleday (1977)